Walmart is Costly

Walmart is Costly

Jasmine Bell

Published by Tablo

Published in 2022 by Tablo Publishing.

Publisher and wholesale enquiries: orders@tablo.io

20 21 22 23 LSC 10 9 8 7 6 5 4 3 2 1

Table of Contents

Books

We all need someone who will tell us the truth and save us time, money, and energy. This person must also provide enough evidence that you cannot refuse them and can benefit from them. Is there less than a 10% chance that your book will be published? According to editors and publishers, there is only a 1–2% chance of it being published. In other words, for every 100 manuscripts they receive, publishers only take one or two, yet on average, books in America only net less than a couple of hundred. It's funny how writing We all need someone who will tell us the truth and save us time, money, and energy. This person must also provide enough evidence that you cannot refuse them and can benefit from them. Is there less than a 10% chance that your book will be published? According to editors and publishers, there is only a 1–2% chance of it being published. Instructors and publishers overlook that, which is useful information. It's not just. In other words, for every 100 manuscripts they receive, publishers only take one or two, yet on average, books in America only net less than a couple of hundred. It's funny how writing instructors and publishers overlook that, which is useful information.

It's not just about knowledge; it's also about execution. Are you tired of digging through your wallet to find some spare change for public transportation or a toll? If not, I still want more from you. It is time for you to begin living a rich life as soon as possible, which will require you to be my financial client and me to be your financial coach. You are already saving a lot of money and on your way to making a lot of money because a financial coach can cost anywhere from $100 to $300 per hour. I'm giving you a fresh chance to learn about core aspects of tallies and totals that will significantly enhance your quality of life. My achievements include, but are not limited to, consistently filing my own taxes, being more financially independent and stable after resigning from my job without another job at age 31 and being able to receive acceptance through an interview into a private Catholic university, Felician University. I know about a 1031 exchange and deferred sales trust due to 90% of millionaires investing in real estate.

Yates, "90% of the World's Millionaires Do This to Create Wealth."

Seagraves, "Your Odds of Getting Traditionally Published – Donny Bailey Se

"Odds Of Being Published - Fiction Writer's Mentor."

Piersanti, "10 Awful Truths About Publishing - Berrett-Koehler Publishers."

Perhaps you're in a situation like Jill Scott's, where your job is gray, and others call you "young and idealistic." On the other hand, you might be one heck of a baseball player, like Art Rust Jr. said he was in so many words, but racial barriers back then held him back. Seeing as how the Modern Baseball League is mostly Hispanic, maybe you feel like even though you legally can become a baseball player, you can't see yourself there because of how they tend to scout. Jill Scott became everything from a songwriter to an actress. She began as a teacher, and she wondered if Jackie Robinson hadn't been in the negro league instead of him by the time, he was older. He substituted by becoming a sports journalist since he couldn't play sports. If and when you are, stop playing mind games and stop playing with your reproductive system, and realize that if you substitute, you better substitute in a way that still surpasses a lot of others who fulfilled your dream but didn't make it to the heights that you will. A cost-effective life affects your life. When we think of a risk-reward assessment, I assert that it is far riskier to spend your life thinking that you're free to ruin your and others' lives as long as it's legal, because there are plenty of you out there who thank God, we don't have morality police and thank God we aren't a theocracy.

Inc, *Contemporary Black Biography.*

As for whether we are in a recession, we can always go back and forth if it looks like it does, but how do we know for sure since the mechanics of it have to be officially voted on? You can imagine being in the future and you can read about it in history books. The National Bureau of Economic Research may be the deciding factor but using the unemployment rate to see if we are in a recession or not Some economists judge If the unemployment rate hits midpoint for many months, it could indicate that the economy is in recession. A recession, another way of looking at it, is to slow down the pace of economic activity. Then there are those who follow the principle that GDP and Gross Domestic Product growth must be low. Are you different from everyone you know?

I remember someone telling a former commenter on public that they thought we were in a recession. The original commenter said they both have their opinions and will not argue about it. The strangest thing is that whether you are going through a very difficult time right now, it's definitely not just a poor time and, to put it mildly, never a good time., how do you determine what a recession is? What if they have been in extreme hardship all of their lives? how should they be taken care of? All they do is fixate on a dilemma instead of remediating the ongoing crisis of poverty.

It's time that one of us thought about off-the-books work; now we can have a greater understanding of what leads up to that and what kind of financial system that involves. Does this remind you of the black market? I see the parallels. It'd be in one's best interest to originate a company and deal with slow growth over that route, does this remind you of the black market? I see the parallels. Can you sense us increasing our minds together? I have enough enthusiasm to feel it for you if you haven't already.

Rationing economists say distribution is what the price mechanism determines, but do most people think that distribution is an option to let price decide how scarce money, resources, and services are distributed? Overpriced distributions, often used when distributions are determined by market forces that are considered unequal rations, may also lead to the advent of a black market as humans promote their rations to those inclined to pay an excessive price. If you pay your maid or architect in cash or make an excuse not to notify the government that you have been paid for assistance rendered, you contribute to the black or underground economy. Because such real-time transactions do not usually show up in GDP figures, the black financial system may also suggest that the United States is a lot richer than professional data suggests in the United States and the United Kingdom.

"The Economist."

You don't have to write to learn about the writing process; the same lengths that a writer goes through to create a fantastic book, you should go through to ensure you have a fantastic life. Doesn't knowing what was once written especially for you increase the price of a book? It should, after all.

I've also been kept in hospitals and precincts in various areas, but even I can't say I've had the incredible pleasure of doing my job in a prison like Jane must've since she stated that, despite the fact that she would prefer not to return, she yearns for it. She was an En poste essayist in a vigorously monitored men's jail.

That begs the question: would you say you'd help write in a jail to improve your chances of writing a hit? Corry needed a second job because her pay was inconsistent after her divorce.

She became propelled and referenced how finding a part-time line of work can move scholars. Now and again, you must do the unimaginable to achieve what has been out of your reach. Who might have believed that a safety officer could teach an educated detainee to browse? I wouldn't have brought it up, and you wouldn't have either if she hadn't, to hinder a creative slump.

If the pundits say my book is the worst ever written, in any case, pundits scrutinize, and authors compose regardless of whether their books sell. Am I only representing my well-being, or is my voice being heard? At the point when you read my words, you have heard my voice, and we're holding hands.

Newtown, "Interview with Jane Corry, Author of My Husband's Wife – Book Club Babble."

"Jane Corry on How Working in a Prison Inspired Her to Write a Psychological Thriller."

Individuals matter more than benefits. The emergency takes place according to non-stop business exercises; individuals go back and forth while benefits are meant to improve and be manageable. See, I may not disagree with you about how an agency should function because, from one point of view, the numbers do not adequately summarize it. Most companies do not create cash in their most memorable year of activity; it by and large takes 18 mos. to 2 years for new businesses to begin bringing in cash. Here is a greater perspective.

The remuneration scale relies on the entrepreneur making $40,000 each and every year on a traditional basis in the initial 5 years of activity; pay fees are no longer considered income. Expenses of the Main Year's Pay: Benefit Assuming the combination is positive, the benefit increases. It is adjusted on the assumption that the truly negative value is unknown.

For instance, an agency with income of $100,000 and fees of $60,000 generates a profit of $40,000 each year. Most entrepreneurs, however, overlook the opportunity to profit in their most memorable year; it can take several years to recoup the initial investment.

This is significant. Is it true that you are on the verge of achieving this goal? A true benefit implies that the originators can make a reasonable payment and have enough money on hand to demonstrate a benefit. Perhaps some intricate programming will figure it out for you; if it doesn't, don't be certain. Have you ever noticed how few merchants actually pay their rent? I can perceive how beneficial this shift in manner would be in particular. Practice it several times to appear to continue the month's profits on the first of each month.

"How Long Does It Take to Be Profitable?"
"A Guide for Small Businesses."

Shorter books have a better chance of selling, and lengthy books have had to become shorter in order to keep up. Since we live in such an increasingly expensive high-tech world with various kinds of stimuli and financial literacy is "intimidating," as one worker told me over the phone, shouldn't my financial literacy book have fewer words? Another student who admitted she needs a financial literacy book initially made a shrieking noise when the topic arose.

Since I'm aware of this as an amateur author, rest assured that I know plenty about finances. Society and you deserve to know too.

How much proof do I need to submit before someone decides this can't be a coincidence?

Browse around. Bookshops of all sizes are closing far and wide, which indicates leisure reading isn't as popular as it once was.

The median bestseller span shows a decline over time, with a 32-page drop from 2018 to 2021.

Dollar cost averaging, stock bits and how to avoid accidentally leaving any in a stock when selling, stock splits, reverse stock splits, and when it comes to executing orders, it all comes down to basic math. You can watch the charts go up and down simultaneously, just as you can see statistical data in the stock market app. Since a stock split involves addition, a reverse stock split involves ratio division. Stocks can be delisted, cashed out, and taxed differently as a day trader than as a retail investor, and day traders are more likely to become wealthy over time.

A lot of you can find out how your company is doing just by seeing if the SEC (the security exchange) has anything to do with it at all. You can watch the charts go up and down simultaneously, just as you can see statistical data in the stock market app. Since a stock split involves addition, a reverse stock split involves ratio division. Stocks can be delisted, cashed out, and taxed differently as a day trader than as a retail investor, and day traders are more likely to become wealthy over time.

"Why best-selling books are getting shorter (msn.com)"

Since we live in such an increasingly expensive high-tech world with various kinds of stimuli and financial literacy is "intimidating," as one worker told me over the phone, shouldn't my financial literacy book have fewer words? Another employee who admitted she needs a financial literacy book initially made a shrieking noise when the topic arose.

There is a world outside the publishing industry that the industry needs to reach, and it is the market where beta readers most closely resemble the market demographic.

If the world hates you, hold on to the idea that it hated me first.

John 15:18

Tucker Max is a bestselling author, ghostwriter, and the founder of Scribe Media. He eventually planned to commit suicide but refused to accept a 500,000 donation from him. He was initially rejected 100 percent of the time and was once told that he couldn't even write an email. Literary dealers who have previously been incorrect are frequently incorrect now.

Editors and literary agents are a must, and they do rather enhance the quality of work, like it or not, due to the fact that we often cannot streamline authorship, and naturally, it's easier working with them.

Yet, if they are not makers, who died and made them king or queen?

Editors are choosy readers, and it stands to reason that literary marketers are even more so because they tend to precede them. What both mechanically neglect is how effortlessly sellable even poorly written books are; they additionally underestimate how without difficulty they end up on the best-seller list.

"Bible hub"

May, "Planned Parenthood Rejects $500,000 from Tucker Max."

"Tucker Max."

I have honestly done my best to make this book as regional as possible, although I will admit I get a lot of inspiration, as you can tell from the various sources, I keep an eye on—that's for our mutual good, of course. I want this book to be sturdy and have a great hold on you. I hope you can keep up with the pace of this book, and I hope you do not become overwhelmed with information just as we start off on this voyage together.

If the following has to do with you I don't look down on you because since you are here for me, I am going to be here for you and we are going to get better together in spite of ourselves, one way to tell the general reader, who is completely oblivious to proper verbiage in the publishing industry, is to use the word regurgitate instead of curate, that even the biblical writers had Jesus as their muse. If a writer is uninspired, then they have writer's block, and that makes them wiser than an overly critical reader when they are smart enough to understand how to better draw wisdom from those wiser than themselves.

Humbly concentrating on the writing process, still deals with money due to a perceived value which I intimately grasp, A person must not only have a consumer surplus instead of a budgetary one. Please look at it the same way you would look at an economics class and read other books besides this one. You do not have to be an economist to read an economics book. Whether or not you hire or become an economist one day, it is just one of those things where, in case it matters, instead of just going with your gut feeling, you could see if his or her actions are in line with what the job entails because you know the ends and ends.

Hitler burned the books; this country is burning down, and it all burns me up. The same people who say a robot will replace their job don't mind voicing that on a computer.

The robot is the problem the problem is that you don't have a backup plan and you always need a backup plan. It doesn't matter whether your job is replaced by a robot or whether your company's been brought out. You are unfocused and undisciplined when you think like that. So, relax and be more refined. Customers pay extra for refinement; think of refined Foods they'll pay more for restaurant quality food even when the food is not good for them. Perhaps you have some toxicity that you have to work on and maybe you have a brain handicap, the point is you need to think about assets and liabilities and use whatever you need to use to be able to easily remind yourself. When we think about full coverage car insurance and then we think about the bare minimum being liability. We have a better idea of how collecting sneakers is still not holding its weight in the more abundant sector like artwork. in Slavery they didn't want the slaves to read.

Hitler burned all books that weren't about Nazism, he burned the books that were Albert Einstein to Marxism yet how can Democrat and republicans today not get along over accusatory Marxism and have racial tensions igniting division? We must come together and rise up above this. This is spiritual anarchy overtaking us.

I know that things out of our control happen, but you can at least try to avoid being a single mother or father or spending up your money on going to restaurants over cooking at home, shopping at thrift shops for the same kind of clothing you would pay more for elsewhere or even better benefit from one of those clothing drives which can end up being featured in a church or food pantry. Returning to the single parent part there is a combination of incomes in the household and there is more stability for the offspring which I came out of, and I will say that from an economic vantage point if you would like to see my point made, keep on reading. Yes, a person can be an abundant single parent just like analogically how a person can go to prison and end up being richer than when they went in. which I have heard of but more likely than not it will not be the result. Earning a career credential online for free. Google offers free learning as does IBM. Stanford also offers free learning. Learning for free over an paying an exorbitant tuition for education even with financial aid that is still money spent that might not have to be. It is not always mandatory to go to college trade school or have an apprenticeship. A college student who has a teacher for a mother can still get financial aid while obtaining prolonged education as a former lover told to me.

I'm not going to urge you to get a luxury car that depreciates in value just because but I will tell you if that's the only way to get you motivated to make as much you can then so be it, just like how it would be better for you to end up living in an apartment nearest college than it is to have to pay for dorm, even though owning a home is always better. I have heard the saying that if you want to hide something from a Black person put it in a book, last I checked it varies but around 5% of Black people are authors. Well, I am beating the odds when it comes to that, and I ought to swim too. Be willing to pay the money that you need to fork over to save your own life, people have the nerve to say do not fight a thief over your money because it is not worth your life when money is inherently for survival and effects your quality of life. Well then it stands to reason that if you must decide between being unhoused during a winter advisory or resorting to living with your family in a home when a lot of people say that you're too old for that, people will point out your problems without giving a solution, do you think that your critics will grieve if you pass away during the winter advisory? They do not even have your best interest in mind while you are alive.

Broad range taxation

The bible speaks on taxes as well and it is righteous to include it here.

Romans 13:6-7

6 For because of this you also pay taxes, for the authorities are ministers of God, attending to this very thing. 7 Pay to all what is owed to them: taxes to whom taxes are owed, revenue to whom revenue is owed, respect to whom respect is owed, honor to whom honor is owed.

I found up to 25 biblical verses on paying taxes.

I have never heard a single sermon on paying taxes in any faith.

If you want to save money start coupon stacking or using fetch do not decide you aren't going to pay taxes.

I do not use lack of reparations for the enslavement of my ancestors as a Black woman to not pay taxes.

Taxpayer dollars go towards a school system that failed to teach me about how during the holocaust Black people were locked up isolated and slain.

Will you end up like Todd Chrisley screaming out to God (Jesus Christ) after tax evasion, sentencing?

Will you end up like Malcolm X turning Muslim after imprisonment for burglary?

What will be your turning point? You must decide today and act by tomorrow.

Take it one day at a time sure tomorrow is not guaranteed to us but you want to give yourself a day to sleep on it. When it comes to crime though as a rule of thumb, it is always best to start right away. The more severe the crimes the worse off we end up, who has the money for bail?

Tax fraud is just not worth it.

"25 Bible Verses About Paying Taxes (ESV) - RANKED."

You may have the option to deduct both organizational and non-organizational costs from the dreaded debt tax deduction. You can clearly distinguish between the non-business commitment portion of Structure 8949 and the dreaded business commitment portion of Timetable C Structure 1040. I unequivocally ask you to confirm the seriousness of this thought.

You should also be aware of the research and development tax relief. Wineries tend to obtain it because it requires trial and error. I agree that each of you should know these costing principles and rules to stay alert to this day. You want to keep doing what you are doing because your name will be on the bill, so you can be seen as competent. Others will not care if you are good at cutting taxes; I can promise you that many of them have not even been taught about it, and assuming they have data on it, chances are they will charge for their broadcast. I understand I am charging for the book, but there is so much you are missing, and I should have a choice.

Topic No. 453 Bad Debt Deduction | Internal Revenue Service (irs.gov)
Are you Qualified, and How to Calculate the R&D Tax Credit (windes.com)

No matter the reality which you are as of now in addition alongside than you have been previously, it might be lamentable assuming which you needed to pay for assist. I can give the statistics however right here so that you can get to it at your rest.

This affects the differences listed between IRS Accountants, CPAS Accountants, and Tax Attorneys. Tax preparation providers are not limited to this list.

A tax return preparer situates and calculates income tax returns on behalf of an individual or business. Accountant

Accountants keep track of transactions and examine ledgers.

Tax attorneys represent individuals and businesses on tax matters. They present options and understand tax laws and possible taxes. CPAS stands for auditors recognized as joint auditors by state audit boards under state law. A person who prepares and calculates income tax returns for individuals and corporations

Enrolled agents are the most knowledgeable in taxes, tend to be the best and most economical tax preparers, and are federally recognized. In the essence of fairness, you still have to choose who is best for you and your situation. I, as a financial coach, am not the same as a financial advisor, but that doesn't mean that I can't size up a client's economic situation, give sound advice, and that a client can't decide that it is more suitable to choose me over a financial advisor in spite of any legal restrictions.

See Distribution 17 if you have any desire to know the amount you ought to pay to try not to cheat on charges. We perceive that a considerable number of you are employed and might be guardians. You have the option of lowering the amount of government fees you wish to pay. The amount of credit you receive is determined by your pay and the number of qualified costs you guarantee. If you have not guaranteed your kid's tax break yet, you have the opportunity. Visit your internet-based account. At the point when you access your internet-based account, you will be furnished with a connection to see your all-out prepayment sum.

The Youngster Tax Reduction Update Gateway is not dynamic at this point. If you have not applied for the kid tax reduction yet, there's still time, so act now before it is past the point of no return. In any case, you can see that your prepayment is complete in your web-based account.

This page gives that connection. Businesses can take part by meeting the qualification prerequisites for the work opportunity tax reduction. We will provide data on this too. Generally, discussing weather conditions classifies as a light diversion; however, when a cataclysmic event occurs, things cease to be frivolous. Typhoons are something we all deal with, so please keep in mind that discounts will be expedited if you document a changed statement in a space where the disaster has been declared. It should mention somewhere in the text, heads up: The IRS is also happy to charge government-overseas retirees who earn more than $25,000 per year.

"IRS Reminds Taxpayers Their Social Security Benefits May Be Taxable | Internal Revenue Service."

"Internal Revenue Service | Work Opportunity Tax Credit."

"About Publication 17: Your Federal Income Tax (For Individuals) | Internal Revenue Service."

"Sign In."

"Tax Credits and Deductions | USA.Gov"

I find it fascinating how we only hear about student loan forgiveness.

Have you heard about college students saving cash by using taxes? You need to research this like a research paper. I received a refund after exiting college in my first semester, and I would never advocate any person like me stay in college, but from an enterprise standpoint, I have respect; I additionally recognize there are enterprise ranges; and I care about you as a person.

In twenty twenty-one it was predicted; Pupil debt would hit one hundred seventy-five trillion and its handiest going up college students and families can maintain extra coins with college tax credit and deductions. Different training-associated tax blessings encompass unique monetary financial savings payments and monetary financial savings bonds college students and families can maintain extra coins with college tax credit and deductions university. Withinside the US treasured in line with the country wide middle for training signs lessons and charges totaled a median of 8620 at public in-kingdom campuses 19034 at public out-of-kingdom universities and 29371.

At personal nonprofit universities for the duration of the 2019-20 instructional yr., to redeem credit score you need to use shape 8863, you will additionally want shape 1098-t, which ought to be mailed to the pupil from the faculty and indicates how a great deal you paid in lessons and certified charges. That year, the Yankee chance tax credit score, the American Opportunity Tax Credit (AOTC) offers a most annual financial savings of 2500 consistent with eligible student in eventual unspecified time in the future withinside the first four years of university. What's top notch concerning the AOTC is that it is far refundable as much as forty so even though the credit score rating you get preserve of brings your tax criminal obligation right all the way down to 0. You could nevertheless stand up to forty of what stays as much as one thousand, the lifespan looks at deposit is akin to the AOTC however it is far substantially much less restrictive this residue is for licensed instructions and related charges paid via way of means of eligible university college students attending qualifying schools.

Gaffney, "Tax Breaks for College Students and Parents | Best Colleges."

"About Publication 970, Tax Benefits for Education | Internal Revenue Service"

Stocks

If you want to know what my dividends look like, I will paint a picture for you. My last dividend on Landa was for 5 cents. I feel like until you own physical real estate, you should prepare by owning digital real estate. In Landa, you learn about how your rental properties are going, but it surely has its flaws. I almost left, just like I almost left Sofi. Just so you know, if your brokerage firm becomes insolvent, most likely your cash will switch to another brokerage firm, but there are steps taken to guard your investment. I will let you know that even though digital real estate is nuanced, traditional investment dividends can be around the same amount as digital, although they are displayed differently. The best way to see how it looks is to try it out; just keep in mind that with Landa, you have to wait for your share to sell and if you cancel, you lose it; and my last dividend from fidelity was 15 cents, so when I look at my SOFI, I don't see a dividend; instead, I see my recent active investing as a cent. Active investing is when you participate in investing, purchasing, or marketing securities to take advantage of brief price fluctuations. I also see an offer to open a savings account with a minimum and get a bonus with a certain APY, which is money you get back on a savings or checking account. So, this is what you have to look forward to.

One bad habit, I've noticed in me, and I've noticed in others is of constantly saying I can't afford it instead of double checking whether they can afford it in the first place and if they can't afford it as Robert Kiyosaki taught you have to do what you have to do in order to get what you need to get. Similarly, At Whole Foods the food sampler gave me a coupon for a free item, and I instinctively said I do not think I have the money then she reminded me how she literally gave me a coupon for something free. if you do not know how to count your money correctly try giving the incorrect amount to a friend and see how fast they teach you how to count correctly. When the teacher fails to teach you and the professor fails to teach you and your parents fail to, try a friend, and know when to seek God. Averaging down in stocks is when you keep buying stocks as the price dips, but it can backfire when the stock keeps losing so you might have to leave the position.

Instead of only adding + subtracting with money you must account for multiplying and the division. Something you do not see people doing is studying word problems for the dual factor of the linguistic composition and the arithmetic component. How would an arithmetic logic unit be of benefit without math? Arithmetic Logic Unit (ALU) is the math and rationale in our computer system.

Besides the common chart that looks like a medical graph there is a circular shaped chart that you can see in a fidelity account, which is like the chart for a logo for a circular economy and a circular economy is rubbish out, preserving products functionality, planning reuse. The round Chart is above a line that will tell you how your investment strategy looks. it says mine looks like a short-term investment strategy, even though I am for the long term because my investments are not heavily weighted in any company. As far as public goes works pending, completed, tips, canceled, rejected, transfers, bonuses, dividends, and trust, invites and subscription. Now select firms like TD Ameritrade which I do not like. Operates better on a computer rather than the phone, none of what I say here as far as these different brokerage firms should prevent you from going whichever one you choose to go with. I also do not like we bull but like their promos. Just like there's people that do not like the teasers for XXX rated content and then there are of those that celebrate it. On a side note, just in case you were wondering the explicit videography industry makes its money off advertising, yet there are still too many companies out there especially small companies that want to keep going with word of mouth from family and friends alone and have those people volunteer for them. Charles Schwab shows U.S./Europe/Asia/Pacific indices on the PC. Fidelity has voice recognition technology.

What you want to know is how a brokerage firm works and I will tell you one thing expect taking on an exit fee. just like you can expect to have to utilize technology when you go on any of these apps for investing instead of like before I was born and paying a stockbroker to execute the order, speaking of which you can expect to pay 1 to 2% value of your assets to the broker nowadays. Since the fees fluctuate in this case you are going to want to shop around. The exit fee can be from 50 bucks to 100 bucks. Transferring your money from a brokerage firm is not the same thing as transferring your money from a bank. A brokerage firm is the intermediary. Brokerages end up summarizing how come they charge their customers what they charge based off the paperwork and transferring data collected about transactions. Before you go with the mutual fund pay attention to the rate of the 12B -one fee

Fee can be up to 75% and overall customers can end up paying a ton.

Basically, This again ties into operational cost. so, we might as well be their employers as the customers because as you can see you are paying employees repeatedly and this is not only in this industry but across the board so you better make sure you are getting the best customer service that money can buy. The 12b-one fee is an embedded part of the fund package.

These are the 5 basics everyone should know when investing. There are two types of parking: legal and illegal. what is legal the act or practice of investing in low-risk and/or highly liquid securities when deciding where to invest in the medium to long term. For example, you can deposit money in government bonds or savings accounts when making these decisions. Illegal activity is the illegal holding or financing of shares on behalf of another party for the purpose of disguising that party's ownership. Parking occurs when an investor owns 5% or more of his outstanding shares and is required to register certain information with the SEC. Parking is a tactic used by corporate predators who want to hide their intent to acquire a company.

Thus, attackers enlist the help of someone else by asking them to hold or fund a certain amount of equity. Here is a breakdown of the key points you should know. Get a complete look at what, where and how your company is doing. Find the company's price-to-earnings ratio, or the current stock price to earnings per share. Corporate betas show stocks carry a higher level of risk compared to the rest of the market. If you want to save money, invest in high yielding stocks. It can be difficult to read but look for the simplest clues in charts such as stock price movements.

"Parked."

"5 Essentials You Need to Know About Every Stock You Buy."

Even if bond and stock fees hit a near-term bottom due to international drinking, epidemics, and violence, there is no need to depress financial investments. What is particularly authentic here is that you're likely to have a broader economic component and a long-term view. You can buy retail bonds, executive bonds, corporate bonds, and closeouts through related investment brokerage services. I personally participate in Charles Schwab and his finance some indicators of steep slopes in his SOFI. But these finances are in the heyday of investment firms operating numerous agencies, clever or not, to meet demand and provide a real bulwark to U-turn knowledge.

Like the other stocks on this checklist, the only way to buy chip stocks is through an internet brokerage. You must pay a good amount of your dues before you notice an insignificant increase in tip and quota. Conversely, if you buy stocks that do not pay dividends, you must accept the problems of Google, Apple, and others. How to choose the safest investment CDs that are in arrears differ from savings debt in that they usually have high per-unit fees, are short-term, and have a so-called fixed term. Plutarch's Markets Fund, a fixed benefit investment firm that also invests in short-term credit bonds, asked Basic. Investment finance linked to cryptocurrencies, all types of equity forms of alternative investments, executive bonds, and equity alternatives.

Davis and Yochim, "12 Best Investments Right Now for Any Age or Income - NerdWallet."

"Certificate of Deposit - Wikipedia."

"What Are Money Market Funds? - Fidelity."

Investors frequently make prognostications about the future, and when they do, that frequently leads to trends. When someone is bullish about commodities, that means they are in anticipation about them, while when someone is bearish about commodities, that means they are fretting about them.

During times of war, it is important to cache defense inventories. An exchange-traded fund (ETF) is a clever way to do this because of the backing by a large number of stocks. The person has a successful history and is veritably fat. The client is a well-funded company that has a history of paying its bills on time. The bulk of the company's income comes from one client, America.

The ETFs end up regulated by the American government.

When there's war, companies that make things like munitions and networks are important.

Whiteman, "Best Defense Stocks of 2022: Defense Investing 101 | The Motley Fool."

Morrison, "Want to Be a Millionaire? Here Are the Best Lottery Games to Play."

Banking

I have never heard a college student, or a college graduate tell me of how they learned to apply for student credit cards or learned about no fee banking apps like MOS for students in college. There are countless college students out there that have no idea how college accreditation works. It is your money, and you should know where it is going and how money spent works accrediting agencies determine a colleges accreditation. Everything ends up being business somehow someway. Ranging from 2018 to now fifty-one % of college students dropped out because of the expenses which is the same amount that are opting for online college because it is more economical. I have also noticed how 51% of ephebic students backed free tuition. From year to year the same number of students and for what? Regional accreditation is more meddlesome as opposed to national accreditation which is less evasive. There appears to be a larger percentage of regionally accredited colleges even though a lot of bible schools for instance are only nationally accredited, yet there seems to be more preachers who are not lay preachers if want to get technical about it instead of being politically correct then there would be a lot of preachers who wouldn't be able to preach anyway. Man, changes but God does not. The bible is immutable.

I will list my sources, but will you list yours? What is your driving force right now?

So many people crave original opinions over reported facts and vice versa. We need both.

Wlodarski and Miller, "What Is College Accreditation? How Does It Work? | BestColleges."

Hess, "51% of Young Americans Support Tuition-Free Public College."

Scipioni, “51% of College Students Dropped out of School Due to Costs, Study Finds.”

I'm a big fan of banking, but I don't recommend banks that want to technologize inaptly. I had a hard time getting a new debit card because of the new system. Also, I had to pay for my phone bill in a different way, which wasn't right and can result in fees elsewhere. Everything was done in a hurry while pretending it wasn't a big deal. Banks have made many mistakes, but they cannot hide from the truth. Of course, there is nothing wrong with credit cards.

You're new to opening a bank account and don't want your credit card to hide your financial problems. But do you know how it can go wrong? Because in this case it is not. There is a product called Emulsion Interest. Naturally, it is distinct from exponential growth.

Nevertheless, we are opting for the highest, we have not arrived yet. Nevertheless, if sustainability is to be attained, we should function to it. If you do not have a cost financial savings account or if your actual checking account makes bit rate of passion and you wind up obtaining a totally free inspect, this is an escape. Since it implies you approve much less. I do not wish to spend a great deal; however, it is alright if you do not misuse it. so, you can remain to produce rate of passion as it normally builds up.

Interestingly, whether you have a financial balance or are commencing one, it is your responsibility as a client of your bank to know how your bank is bringing in cash with the goal of producing greater cash stream. Your bank earns money by means of lending your money to others and charging them premiums and defalcation prices. it is a wise stream to mortgage cash to others with an association while any other person is in a settlement and has apprenticed to repay you that money, which in flip includes risk but cuts the risk. often speaking, you hold that the accord can be greater academic than may be anticipated. main belong. attempted Lendee, nonetheless it did not work. if they have advantages or pay but still crave credit, which you could examine them and accommodate with them. Regardless of what the doubter says, the financial transaction rarely is a Ponzi arrangement, if you are still apprehensive placing your money there. likewise, the bank deposits money into dossier reserve(s).

Neither the inventory exchange nor a Ponzi arrangement exists. How are banks placing money from their valued clientele right into a Ponzi arrangement to increase their own wealth? I do not feel so.

There is also an inventory marketplace in different nations. in case you choose to ignore it, you would stronger launch thinking about land. the manner that this massive variety of banks be offering domestic mortgage advances: accommodation is staying placed, and leasing brings in cash despite whether you cannot sell.

It's fine to receive a postal order for paying money if you must, but continually having to depend on help is not ideal. It reminds me of how society is the one who plays the lottery but never buys stock exchange; not entirely in a bank, you frequently take interest, but in a linked to the internet extreme yield lending institution report, you receive an elevated rate.

Let me request this: Other than the bank, what additional alternatives do you have? You can select a limited bank or an abundant one—it all depends on your necessities. You can sustain services by cashing checks or escaping checks, and it's more reliable. Bank reports are simpler to open than credit union reports, and the government's lenient offerings—while there is nothing wrong with accompanying credit unions and hospitality—are more varied when we are required. You can retreat by bearing arranged transactions with the bank and thus working your habit until you find additional commercial records that fit your behavior and will help you meet your objectives.

The FDIC ensures your services until $250,000. Actor and musician Jason Weaver, who rejected two heaps for $100,000, must yield as well as he pretended. Opening a savings account can assist you in cultivating your figure, desiring success, and being systematized, and whatever it takes to bring those two things together. Simply making a deposit and being capable of saying, "I have unlocked a checking account as an adult, and I feel so adult immediately," can display superior idea abilities. Although Fidelity is not a bank, they can assist you in avoiding bounced checks and disbursements.

"Singer From Original 'Lion King' Turned Down $2 Million & Took Royalties Instead."

Tyler Cowen, an American financial specialist recognized that financial aspects is universal.

Insightful money matters can shield us from not improving plus aid us in good decision making and lead to us having jubilant lifespans.

The final purpose of the financial side is to observe and promote the enhancement of nicely-being. Ben Bernanke, the onetime Chair of America Federal Reserve, was integrated with him in that recognition. Who can contend with that? Our Internal revenue Service is presently stockpiled, and I am aware of how evident 2017 was from today, however can you imagine if America implemented this degree? In 2017, a theorist in behavioral economics, Richard Thaler, acquired the noble laureate in Economics for his groundbreaking work on the "nudge" concept.

The way small-scale activities promote individuals to make distinct selections is mutually groundbreaking and debatable. for this cause, the accumulation of many individuals will bring about widespread adjustments to the economy and society. the United Kingdom authorities, for instance, these days began sending tax notices in handwritten envelopes. This simple " personal" contact has ended in a further £ two hundred million in sum unpaid a year. The African monetary Fund is the monetary institution intended by using the African Union, however through the years its commitments could be transferred to the African principal bank. The institution is one in every of three destiny African Union monetary institutions. established in Yaoundé, Cameroon We pay attention plenty approximately Africa, however lamentably maximum of it is bleak, ignoring the advantageous monetary traits, inclusive of the prospect of an applicable and feasible African monetary Fund. From now until the destiny, timing is the entirety, and economics will continually play an important function. What if you got the chance to see all this stuff up close and private? Why not you? I hope this incentivizes aspiration. We have to figure out a method to bridge the space.

Murphy, "What Is the Future of Economics?"

Upon reflection consider how many times you felt that you had no choice but to not read a book at all or end up skipping to the most vital parts. Nothing else mattered; all that mattered was your reasoning, and sure, you still passed that exam or quiz or got your license, but you couldn't have possibly felt as accomplished if you had just read the entire book. What counts more, accomplishment or being rich? We can become accomplished in several ways.

Notice how a job will have an employee of the month, so employees are unaware that they are wasting their time being at that job. Before the invention of money, goods and services were exchanged through barter and the use of commodities such as salt, livestock, and grain. In fact, in 5000 B.C., people used metal objects as a means of payment to exchange goods and services. us in 1690, banknotes represented letters of credit or promissory notes. In 1996, a new currency was introduced in the United States to finance the civil war. One thing I learned at Bergen Community College was that there is a time and place for skimming when reading. As is common knowledge, what distinguishes the rich from those who are not is how much more they make in less time. It's funny how IOUS and credit don't equate to cash, yet they are both based on trust, and in God we place our trust, which is our cash.

"Everything You Need to Know about... Bartering."
"When Did the U.S. Start Using Paper Money?"

A hint that we profit from the information we have about the United States early recessions. In April 1960, savings experienced a slump that lasted until February 1961. The frugal lifestyle wasn't as distressing as it had been in the past during the inflation of 1969–1970. According to business-related research, there was a difference in the number of services nations retired from their bank reports in 1969 and 1970, and it lasted longer than usual. The justification for this was a reduction in how much administration was recognized, which made it harder for local areas to get administration. The 1970s slump, from 1973 to 1975, marked the end of Western marketing inactivity and represented the entirety of the typical commercial growth that followed World War II.

It stood out from many previous recessions because extreme inaction accompanied extreme growth and dirty growth. Yes, they occur roughly simultaneously. Expansion A rapid rise in real GDP The real GDP stops rebuilding and begins to fall.

Either under pressure or without pressure, the real gross household income decreases and reaches its lowest point. The real gross household amount then stops decreasing and begins to rise. The 1973-1975 downturns resulted in a period of creative inactivity in many parts of the Western world for the entire 1970s, putting an end to the typical post-World War II fiscal happening. Unlike many previous downturns, this one contained an economic decline in which extreme inactivity and activity coexisted. The term "disaster drop" was coined in 1972 by statistician Solomon Fabricant.

"Growth Recession - Wikipedia."
"Recession of 1969–1970 - Wikipedia."
"1973–1975 Recession - Wikipedia."

Sanctions are undeniable. When talking about monetary history, minister Gino Jennings comes up short on a doctorate in religious philosophy, similar to how God provided him with the endowment of teaching and God provided me with the endowment of monetary preparation and composition.

Minister Gino chastised Obama for calling on Africa to safeguard unfamiliar gay privileges and cautioning them with sanctions while they were jeopardized. President Thomas Jefferson proposed the Ban Demonstration of 1807 to rebuff England and Napoleonic France for pestering our boats toward the end of the second great war. America revived its energy for international restrictions for the purpose of managing world legislative issues. President Wilson asked the American people to assist the group of countries because its endorsing power is an alternative to war sanctions imposed by the collusion that couldn't prevent Italy from attacking Ethiopia in 1935, and so on.

Overall, the United States has reestablished its zeal for international restrictions for the purpose of managing global issues and has asked Americans to assist certain countries on the grounds that its authorizing powers work or different demonstrations of war that led to sanctions in the Second World War have led one nation's activities to obstruct financial trade with various countries to become the answer for each unfamiliar rule issue. President Barack Obama has sanctioned an average of 500 organizations every year, which has nearly tripled during Donald Trump's administration; however, after an age of these approvals, targets are looking for alternatives to the dollar to protect themselves from compulsion. Computerized monetary forms offer one way out for individuals. The People's Bank of China has created a computerized yuan that will enable those who use it to completely bypass the US dollar; indeed, even our European partners supported the instrument on the side of exchange trades, INSTEX, as a method through which they could bypass the dollar and exchange with Iran.

Foreign Affairs. "The United States of Sanctions,"

Pastor Gino Jennings Speaks on Barack Obama - YouTube

From the Dutch tulip lunacy south ocean air pocket to the Mississippi organization trick the American fraudster Sarah Emily Howe who worked Ponzi plans amid the 1870s and 1880s scandalous women installment organization of Boston. Howe was captured in 1880 and detained for a long time for extortion, yet after her release she rehashed comparable fakes until she was captured again in 1888.Could you spot the amount of misnomer in the word "Ponzi" plot name at any point? An extremely chronologically misguided component to it was that Sarah's bank was uncovered as false during a bank run. A bank run is the point at which a ton of bank individuals were arrested. Take out reserves all the while, which carries us to capital flights, which happen when resources or cash quickly stream out of a country because of a monetary concern or as the consequence of a political event.

For example, rule change or globalization happens when resources or cash quickly stream out of a country because of an occasion of financial concern or as the consequence of a political occasion (for example, rule change or globalization) in the period since his seizure. Aug. 12, 1920: Charles Ponzi's name has been associated with the trick that got him sentenced and detained. Ponzi likewise declined to deliver insights concerning his plan of action, similarly to how Bernie Madoff executed his effective money management methodology, guaranteeing that he would rather not impart data to contenders but guaranteeing that he could get it and exchange it at face value with us for large benefits. Ponzi guaranteed financial backers a 50% profit in 45 days and a 100% profit in no less than 90 days, and it appeared as though he was a man who certainly could be trusted, as early financial backers were compensated a lot. He soon had financial backers eager for him to take their cash, but none of it added up. Have you heard about the worldwide financial asset established to a limited extent by John Maynard Keynes? It was formed in 1946 and began on December 27th, 1945, at the Bretton Woods discussion established in 1945 by 29 constituent states. It currently assumes a decisive role in regulating cost issues and major financial emergencies, which Harry Dexter White likewise made the IMF do.

"The History of Ponzi Schemes Goes Deeper Than You Think."

"Capital Flight - Wikipedia." "International Monetary Fund - Wikipedia."

I want to present to you the various ways that addictions cost people money. I hope this will motivate you to beat your addictions because it is too costly and not worth it.

Engel's law

As people grow richer, they can afford better food, so their food spending may increase, but they can also afford frills, so they spend more on the frills. Obesity:

Lost savings potential: obesity can lead to serious conditions like type 2 diabetes.

Diabetes complications can cost up to $1,600 out of your own pocket.

Expenses not covered by insurance If you were able to retain a stronger weight

and block type 2 diabetes, that money, invested for 15 years, could add up to an

estimated $37,000 instead.

Taxes: Uncle Sam currently collects about $180 per American each year in federal

and state income taxes to fund Medicare and Medicaid payments related to obesity.

care. For a family of four, that's about $720.

Health care expenses

Obesity is a major contributor to type 2 diabetes. And the

A typical monthly bill to treat diabetes complications can range from $350 to $900.

without insurance. You could potentially give between $4,200 and $10,800 per year.

out of your own pocket.

Fuel costs—the extra pounds that Americans have put on over the past decade—have

required airlines to use an extra 350 million gallons of fuel, according to analysis by

Cornell University researchers' Total cost to American air travelers: $275 million.

Chronic drug use

The Public Foundation on Chronic Drug Use gauges that the maltreatment of and dependence on nicotine, liquor, illegal medications, and physician-recommended prescriptions financially affects American culture to the tune of more than $700 billion annually.

This figure incorporates medical care costs, lost efficiency, and wrongdoing-related costs. To be honest, the narcotics epidemic alone costs $78.5 billion each year.

Betting:

The Public Committee on Issue Betting estimates the yearly public social expense of issue betting at $7 billion. These expenses incorporate betting-related law enforcement and medical care spending as well as employment cutbacks (see Chapter 11) and different results. This gauge depended on research from the 1999 Public Betting Effect Study Commission to represent expansion and momentum in issue betting.

Hoarding: bills overdue equal penalty fees. misplace checks and even cash. Buy unnecessary things. Spend money on trivial items. Collect multiple items because when you lose what you're looking for, you purchase another one. Rent a storage area for extra space. These habits can create an overall financial problem. Hoarding, even just a little bit, can leave bank accounts empty while homes overflow with unnecessary belongings.

Storing:

Bills that are past due are subject to penalty charges.

lose checks and even money.

Purchase unnecessary things.

Burn through cash on insignificant things.

Gather numerous things since when you lose what you're searching for, you buy another.

Lease a capacity region for additional room.

These propensities can make money an issue in general. Even a small amount of storage can leave financial balances void, while homes become overrun with useless possessions.

Typical Storage Cleanup Expenses

"As a result, storing cleanup administrations can cost $50 to $75 per cubic yard, $50 to 125 per work hour, and $.75 to $2.50 per square foot for cleaning and sanitizing."

Addiction to shopping:

Compulsive shoppers include:

58% are heavily in debt.

42 percent are unable to make their debt payments.

45% feel guilty about their purchases.

33% receive shopping criticism from friends and family.

8% are dealing with financial and legal issues.

8% have criminal legal issues.

Black-Stockham, 2021

"What does overeating really cost?"

"How Much Does It cost to Maintain an Addiction? | Price of Drug Abuse."

"Shopping and Spending Addiction Statistics | What You Should Know."

If you ever fall victim to fraud, the bank will notify you and pay for you to sign up for identity theft software. I know it's scary, and you have every right to be worried about it. However, at this rate, crime is so rampant, as you can see even from the premise of this book, that we get into trouble no matter where we go. Banking with a debit card beats relying on one of those prepaid cards. You can get out of a foreign card fee for spending money abroad; those prepaid card fees, like the one you get when you donate plasma, are a whole different story. You can If your bank is anything like mine, you will be able to see a chart in which you will be able to see when it peaks and when it dips end that chart is useful pay attention to it that shirt is reminiscent of other economic graphs that you will see more of the more involved you get in terms of being economically sound and having that economic preparedness about yourself. Bank smart, work smart accept your bank balance and accept what has to stay in what has to go. Random fact: did you know that insurance from banks costs us money? Yes, it is referred to as Bancassurance. What do you think you will do now that you have both sides and know that I am still in favor of depositories? I hope that whichever choice you make will be ideal for you.

In the early 1930s, folks started hoarding gold due to bank failures, a depressed economy, and a stock market crash. How is it people lived through it and cannot remember or are unaware? We need to read to remind ourselves just as much as to inform ourselves. Look how we acted during the pandemic by hoarding common household items like toiletries. Look how the constitution "Neither slavery nor involuntary servitude, except as a punishment for crime whereof the party shall have been duly convicted, shall exist within the United States, or any place subject to their jurisdiction."

And Black people are disproportionally imprisoned. We were no longer on the gold standard and that had pros and cons, but this seems to not be working out for us. Do you agree or not? Therefore, I and others think that if the U.S. dollar fades out, we aren't going to have crypto as our primary currency and will have a new paper currency like when we went from 10 grand bills to counting it out or after the revolutionary war when congress did away with the continentals. We do not want to risk falling for Forex scams or crypto scams which are both forms of virtual fraud. At one time it was illegal to own gold property. Richard Nixon in 1970's ceased the equalizing of dollar, gold ratio and controlled price earnings and expenses. All of this ends up leading to a global fiat system.

Credit

There is a direct relationship between the association and the consequences of your life. When you go back to when you were conceived and the way you were raised, there is your story, then there is history, which is made up of your mother's story and your father's story, then there is your side, and then there is reality. You should think about how you balance the cost with how you shop, and we have purchasing power. Your spending power can vary with cards like Amex depending on your payment history and credit history. I personally do not even have American Express; I have a Sable and have not received my physical card. Then there is the Tomo card, which does not require you to have a credit score to get approved like the Sable. The problem is that Tomo requests may not get an authorization response when they should. If you have imperfect credit and need to fix it, there are Search Platinum Cards and Aspire Cards that allow you to preselect without jeopardizing your score. Businesses receive a reputation rating just like individuals; there is no questioning how Accompaniment runs its business or how it treats other customers like you. Bond ratings range from 300 to 850.

Maximum businesspeople, other than Dave Ramsey and others like him, consume credit to their talents. I am additionally relating to those businesspeople who were previously broke. A person from a console featured on YouTube advised Patrick that they do not remember why people consume credit cards and would not desire one. an alternate guy at the console brings up OPM, which stands for other people's cash. Patrick Ben-David stated it most appropriate. Patrick Ben-David said it best " But I will tell you amongst people who have money you will see that guys who have real kind of money will not use debit cards and not because they don't have the cash they use the kind of credit cards that you pay at the end of the month I don't know it's like 400,000 or 500,000 dollars a month but we have to pay it every month it's not rolling right? and the reason for that is protection. You don't want your debit card out there." We do not really hear much from those who are rich saying they got there from studying Dave Ramsey what we hear is a lot of people who are not rich following his teachings.

"What Is the U.S.'s Obsession with Credit?"

Words paint pictures and since these follow a pattern, take note. When the time comes, let these terms be like a clock, no matter how indulgent, so you can watch them.

Revolving credit = open bank account with a threshold amount that can be accepted with no time limit for payment

Average life the average length of time a bond issue is counterparty-

should be the exception. Total number of bonds divided

equal to the total number of bonds.

a condition in which the price of an asset or class of assets exceeds its initial value

in a long time. Age of grace - one time period, a

pay one credit line in advance one

finance fee

Unlimited credit = a form of credit that allows a person to use finance to make purchases without a pre-determined prepayment period

Time Value of Money = Relationship between time, tycoon, and rate of return (interest rate) and their effect on earnings growth. The more time the tycoon and interest rates rise, the more profitable the tycoon is at the end of the period.

Desire = detail that a person wants to have but is not necessary for life. Specifics, conditions, or services may improve quality of life, but we cannot live without them.

How does punctuality keep popping up in tax jargon and we keep forgetting to waste time? We must start having an emotional connection with it. We will have one way or another. Do not get so caught up in the grace period or open credit that you forget the due date and do not know if it's the right fit to meet your needs.

You want to be responsible, so as not to be penalized as of recent.

"Financial Literacy Basics and Vocabulary | University of West Florida."

The more you learn, the faster your progress will be. The way the central bank conducts its operations has a big impact on how the securities exchange operates, right? High recurrence exchanging also plays an important role in considering what states can imply for others globally and locally, which influences us here and there. I can see how they can still be connected even though they are currently cut off; doesn't the overall picture become more obvious? Have you ever noticed how frequently these words are used in contexts other than the economy and how closely they relate to our daily lives?

This is because the US economy is directly related to them. Banks and credit affiliations advance to other safe associations unsound transient recoveries at the public authority upholds rate. Low government funds rates make investing in less developed nations worthwhile. Strong monetary planning outside of the US is less appealing due to high government uphold rates. The value of money-related principles is also impacted by rates, with the US dollar's value being extended to a greater extent and the value of other financial structures, such as the Mexican peso, being decreased. Two major long-term objectives for the National Bank are as follows: Control development (sell) falcon and increase work dove (reluctant). The light arrival of the business cycle is the interaction by which the economy moves from development to direct development. It is conceivably consistent as it draws near, but a downturn is possible.

The Federal Reserve is working to adjust seemingly unrelated situations of high-recurrence trading. Cycle to Try not to Hard Land A business cycle is an economy that quickly transitions from high development to low development or sideways as it moves toward a downturn to control expansion. The Federal Reserve's long-term goal is to increase pigeon labor and use raptors to control expansion. Situations that ought to be obvious as problematic are being coordinated by the Federal Reserve. High Recurrence Trading (HFT) deals with large amounts of turnover and exchange requests. A business cycle is the process by which an economy transitions from moderate development to steady development, edging closer to but avoiding a downturn. A hard arriving in a business or business cycle is an economy that quickly transitions from high development to low development or sideways as it heads toward a downturn to contain expansion.

BAJPAI, "Strategies and Secrets of High Frequency Trading (HFT) Firms."

"Hard Landing - Wikipedia."
"Soft Landing - Wikipedia."
"Federal Funds Rate - Wikipedia."
"Hawkish vs Dovish: Differences Between Monetary Policies."

When people cannot get money or credit from lenders or creditors, a credit crunch is experienced. It is like how a recession can make us appreciate our credit privileges. Consequently, Credit Sesame sent me this offer. $255 in a deposit earns you $30. Select Now to View Terms of Service. Make sure you are comfortable with the terms. Even though I have not had a credit card in a while, I always use it responsibly. Before you take any action, observe what is occurring. This is a manufactured equivalent of the phrase. A gift card website presents identical looking contracts, demonstrating the herd mentality. Negotiable offers with financial benefits. See the terms and conditions of the Credit Engineering Promotion and Instant Deposit. reward. There are limitations. No room for an offer. The offer may be changed or discontinued at any time by Direct Open Sesame. A direct member must sign up for Sesame Cash's credit builder program within that time frame and have 1,000 prepaid eligible Sesame members in order to be eligible. Each redemption is restricted to one. By financial institution, direct debit lead times may differ. Direct deposits are distinct from peer-to-peer payment systems, test payments from financial institutions, mobile check deposits, deposit-to-deposit ACH transfers, peer-to-peer payment systems, and money transfer apps. At any time, you can modify or cancel. Instant Deposit Promo: The initial xxx Open Sesame Eligible Member configured Instant Deposit as required. Benefits Paid by Individual Employers, Payroll Providers, or Automated Clearing House/ ACH ("Instant Deposit") Benefits Notice of Offer must be initiated. alternatively, press the relevant call to action. The same is done by debt relief businesses, who trade assets to lower debt. It is good, but not the best, to pay off debt.

"Sesame Cash Incentivized Offer Terms - Credit Sesame."

As of 2022, there are fines for being unsecured in Massachusetts, New Jersey, California, Rhode Island, and the District of Columbia. If you don't have a fitness insurance plan you need it so that your insurance can cover medical charges as an alternative of paying out of pocket,

The first step is to ask the vendors to send you an itemized consignment listing all the services

These files must include a line-by-line list of all the charges. Please overview them carefully and look for coding mistakes, double charges, and unsuitable calculations.

Ask the vendors if they offer any economic aid, charity programs, or medical debt forgiveness. Be trustworthy about your circumstance and prepare to make extra cellphone calls and grant documentation to determine your eligibility for some assistance programs. If this does not work out, you can ask about compensation plans.

The choice is yours though I admit that I am not rushing to get a health care credit card myself and can understand why you would not. Medical credit cards need to be Last Resort because they can become overwhelming.

You should always pay with cash a debit card or check.

I, on the other hand, think that as long as you know in advance that you can pay it back in full on time and there is 0% interest and understand the terms of the plan, I don't think it's a bad idea the choice is yours, although I have to admit I'm in no rush to get a health credit card and I can see if you haven't.

"NFCC - National Foundation for Credit Counseling - Home."

Norris, "Is There Still a Penalty for Being Uninsured in 2022?"

Little things accumulate

In our view of the inner city, spotting the scattered debris, abandoned buildings, expelling bodily fluids or public intoxication, from hand me downs to bootleg designer wear and more, these seem like small things separately and can easily not be picked up on to those desensitized to it or willfully oblivious. To others living within the measured comfort and false security of their neighborhoods and mainly those unfamiliar with this way of life, this serves as a virtual guide where the image is in the mind and the collection that separates our region from the suburbs and rural areas and are like bus zones.

God is the ultimate author, and he gave us free will to be the author according to his will for us lives refusal to accept him as the sovereign being that he is, through mistaking ourselves for being the only ones responsible for our own life and thus transferable, with far-reaching consequences when we act. we also must edit parts of our life and clean up the script, or more precisely, the methods to shape our lives. People judge a book by its cover and read, praising, or criticizing or silently sizing up, and people throw around the phrase support system, which matches publishers across the country.

Companies are like our lives made up of people just like us.

Any entity for profit or non-profit earning and getting tax credit operating as a business logically is one and paperwork has left no room for doubt and is inarguable.

To put it simply Volunteering and charity have their pros but be reasonable when building wealth, no matter how painful it is. This also applies to tithes and offerings, the church is still a business, so make sure they are doing the right thing.

I have a secret to tell you: Technology makes the gap wider between the rich and the raggedy.

If you want your own "rags-to-riches" story, then pay attention and keep up.

Receiving a good education is no longer sufficient, nor is landing a high-paying job. Making money off land does not beat tech.

There are still hunters and gatherers who can attest.

how it is insufficient. During the hunter-gatherer age, humans made a bigger deal out of nature and did not debate global warming.

If you study computer science, you must know what kind of math will be utilized.

You might know about calculus or algebra, binary mathematics, college algebra, statistics, discrete mathematics, performance analysis, Graph Theory, Linear Algebra, Function Notation, Probability, and combinatorics (which is a technicality), all of which are known to contribute to coding, but that doesn't mean you will need to know all these things in order to be able to be an effective coder. I just want to encourage you to become more familiar with these components in general.

I used to use HTML codes for websites.

I hope you find this interesting and helpful.

Brooks, Thron, and Ph.D., "What Kinds of Math Do I Need to Know for Coding? Wyzant Blog."

Bonfligo, "Coding for Kids."

"What Kind of Math Is Used in Computer Programming."

Stop wasting time fighting preventable diseases. A clever way to solve this is to show self-love and take care of yourself. Statistics vary by age group and grammatical rules governing nouns that imply gender or sensuality, but the average person has two to four colds per period. I have my own health issues and still cannot beat it. Do not wait for glamorous care. The average person spends four hours a day grooming. I am sure my chances of being present have diminished, but I am curious why you can know that now. You had it in mind because you were doing it. Do not spruce up your dog too much. It only takes 20 minutes. Dogs have feelings too. Look, give your dog a break and take care of yourself. Take extra time for yourself. the dog is fine Prompt your dog and imagine how it barks. It is a sign. Stop wasting your time because you are temporarily on a downward path. Coupled with the potential options that come with it, it is a desperate case to solve.

If a person is useless to you, do not hang out with them. They cannot even help themselves, so what can they offer you? Nothing.

Trott, "How Long Does It Take to Groom a Dog?"
"People Average 4 Hours a Week on Personal Grooming. Why?"

A vital element of the school day is that maximum change programs (artsy type) are well known subjects which can be part of core look at, at the same time as athletic programs are extracurricular applications. As a result, the buying and selling application receives additional guide when the teachers' allowances get paid, whilst the coaches receive payment through the sports activities branch. As a result, seminaries inspire their scholars to improve their instructional overall performance by using allocating acceptable finances to athletic programs. Participating in academy-backed sports is not simplest necessary for fulfillment; It additionally builds self-belief, develops an advantageous mind-set, and teaches the significance of teamwork. While spending on sporting goods, garb, clothing, fitness, and health is inclusive, the sports activities enterprise generates up to $seven-hundred billion yearly, or 1% of global GDP.

Patronage and Licensing Agreements in addition to large media offers and other tangible items like tickets and discounts, expert sports activities corporations and federations additionally make huge quantities of cash by giving sponsors a rights institution to sell items that constitute their league or group. Participating in a team recreation gives most of the equal blessings as becoming a member of a sports group. Cooperation, field, focus and a laugh are only a few of them. As you could see, actively taking part in sports has many blessings, from fitness to body. It also equips the player with the Troubleshooting Wand and the active Wand. Similarly, the game has a fantastic effect on society through decreasing social evils, generating profits and changing society. Experimental formulations and experimental justifications differ. Become a sports rich person and fail at being the pinnacle educate, empathize along with your inner baby, or participate within the vicarious hustle. The maximum usually used kinds of calculations in chemistry include algebra, graphs, numbers, ratios, math, and opportunity. They are accustomed to stabilized chemical reactions, measure molecules, and consider molecular structures, amongst different effects. Chemical calculations must be translated into practical contexts.

"Why Do Sports Get More Funding Than the Arts - Answersdetail.Com."

Helmenstine, "Empirical Formula: Definition and Examples."

The only way to improve your chances of being victorious at the lottery is to purchase a variety of tickets. The intention of the lotto is to cause humans to lose cash to make profits. I am sure it's critical to your socioeconomic advancement and financial well-being to be aware of the arrows impossibility theorem and what it offers with the accepted imperfection of election systems, as well as that the only way to increase your odds of winning the lottery is to purchase a large number of tickets.

You additionally want to be capable of apprehending that when it comes to fundamentals like addition and subtraction, multiplication, and division, you should focus your attention on getting better at them and/or learning them in the view that they will empower you to attain greater factors when it comes to managing your money. Have you ever observed how there are measurements in trend graphs and in the culinary arts? Math can be subjective, just like artwork, when it comes to what we view as relevant to us and how we experience it. Whether you ever become an expert at the fundamentals, you should still prefer learning how others recognize that 9 inches equals .25 with division or 1/4th yard or how forty x four equals one hundred and sixty or how companies like Apple will make their packaging distinctive to get customers excited about opening their packages. Bookkeeping and economic statements are the sorts of matters that get less complicated as we do our best to build up to them. Do not get me wrong, although you can nonetheless be a success when it comes to arithmetic, science, cash administration, and somewhere else. Despite your inability to hold close or in such a manner, all I ask is that you try, so can you try? Please do yourself a favor and try.

A timeworn fella at Walgreens alerted me that the epitome of life is contentment, what amount are you willing to pay to respect life for low pay? So, pay attention to what people say and do. Which do you think is more enjoyable: being filthy rich and living with a budget surplus, or living with a budget deficit and spending what little money he has on fun activities? When I was in high school, she claimed she was kidding around when she said my life was uninteresting because of my lack of exploration due to income limitations but it was true.

How is my life monotonous now as then? Too bad. Because this interesting, we should care about entrepreneurship. You should not be obsessed over suicidal ideations in your life until you have experienced all that life has to offer. How many people do you know who will be legendary? How many famous, rich, or wealthy people are you familiar with? Most people are quick to answer that those type are unknown to them. If you do not love crime or debt, observation makes perfect, so observe success. If you do not start looking for mentors and role models who are outdoing you by a lot, you will never learn how to get offensively rich. That is not what I want for you, but the question is, do you long for it for yourself? You have a choice, so make the best of it.

Biases economical spot

Antimarket bias
Cherry-picking data
Availability bias
sunken cost bias
The understandability biases

Many would say that is a great investment when college is only a security plan and a competition, not to mention you might not get a job in your major or minor, but ignore that, those in higher education need a job, and there is supposed to be help for alumni.

Talk about a double standard.

Many people will remain impoverished because they would rather have a large screen TV with surround sound than a library.

I will give you the definitions, and I want you to guess which goes with which.

a political bias that leads you to not accept policies that are beneficial. Which is?

Antimarket bias

Choosing which evidence to believe in money matters, which Is?

Cherry-picked data.

Which currency cannot be refunded?

The sunk cost data relates to unrecoverable funds.

deciding based on an instance, which is?

Availability bias.

Which iniquity is being rewarded in academia?

Understandability bias.

I never learned the last one in college; it must have slipped the professors' minds.

I try to make this as interactive as possible without being condescending; pardon any unintended disrespect.

I do not seek confirmation bias, and I pay no attention to outcome bias.

Let us unbiasedly vote since there were those, such as my predecessors, who could not.

In terms of BBB accreditation, it is up to the companies listed whether they want to continue to show up on the BBB or not, and it is up to the companies that are not appearing whether they will be accredited or not. What we do not want to do is automatically write off schools because of a BBB accreditation; we want to focus more on complaints against the company, the grade, and how the company responds to complaints. We also want to focus on other businesses that may not want to be featured because a lot of their consumers do not care about it or because they want to cut costs. Every time a company must pay for these kinds of expenses, it somehow causes you to pay extra, the customer. If I decide I am going to launch a business website and I am going to need a funnel to generate leads, I am going to incur a merchant charge of 1.3 to 3.5% on every transaction when it comes to credit processing. Would it be right for me to eat the cost, and what if you decide you will go to my competitor? You can see how this leaves us both in a fix, and then there are swindles out there targeting businesses using free credit card processing to lure them in. If you feel like the owner is charging you incorrectly, I encourage you to see if you can reach a resolution with the company, and if worse comes to worse, you can always contact your Attorney General.

The Germans had been activated via way of means of the planetary commander in racism America bigotry became a financial burden on the United Nations of World War II related to the despondency of 1929-1939, that made the main business occasion of the twentieth century the effect of the conflicts was changed and generally the conflict finished the downturn. The public authority rose out of the conflict as a strong figure with the capacity to direct financial action and control a piece of the economy through spending and utilization during the 1930s. After Japan hit pearl harbor America entered the subsequent extraordinary conflict in December 1941 of each 1942 America state district showed that Nazi Germany expected to butcher every one of the Jews of Europe and in 1943 the American media gave a ton of information of the continued with bloodbath of the Jews.

The U.S. could have gotten different things done to pound the targets of Nazi Germany and its accomplices to save more Jews by then and did not in any case later in January 1944 President Roosevelt empowered the groundwork of a contention exiles board gigantic number of lives have been saved through the undertakings of American trade was upheld by the contention. The us thoroughly enjoyed unrivaled financial and political influence after 1945the division of the vault brought in cash to pay for the contention including through private obligation and war protections charges upheld close to 1368 billion of the struggles fixed expense of 304 billion to cover the other 1672 billion the safe division in like manner extended its security program.

"The United States and the Holocaust, 1942-45."

For the duration of pre-moderate occurrences, people had to adjust to the use of English, Spanish, and French money, while under English rule, we also used pounds, shillings, and pence. The cost was no longer the same in every state, and prior pioneers and native Americans developed a method of exchange utilizing tobacco skins and beaver in addition to wampum and fur. Inflationary pressures influence the Fed's interest rates from time to time. The central bank framework, or what it was responsible for, is defined as follows: It was established following the 1907 panic; it was established on December 23, 1913, following the Fed hold movement; the Federal Reserve is

, after the Federal Reserve's holding movement; the Central bank is the US's major monetary plan. As a result of the wonderful surrender all desire

The public government's power has created considering the monetary emergency of the mid 20s and 1930s

and the exceedingly extraordinary slump of the 2000s, government experts' power has grown. "Obsolete cash" suggests cash other than the public government's paper cash that is given through components that consolidate domain banks. Railroad expert's regions and express lawmaking bodies' country financial association coins have the best number of out-of-date banknotes, otherwise called broken banknotes.

"Obsolete Currency - Perakis Currency."

"Federal Reserve - Wikipedia."

"History of United States Currency | MyCreditUnion.Gov."

Desjardins and Conte, "The History of Money in America: From Beads to Virtual Currency."

When I was in school, I recall being when I had been expelled from my commune and being transferred to another commune. I was never good in school, but that is okay, I just got better by being an autodidact; you might too. My dad was expelled from high school, and my mother had taken bound specialized training classes.

To show how impressive, I once recognized us to be individually and collectively, as well as being a descendent of African slaves and disabled, I decided to look into how slaves were treated. Since it is part of the status quo that we are not physically or mentally fit, we must find a workaround that makes us unique in a specific way.

I had wrongly believed that as soon as their masters learned, they would go berserk and kill them in retaliation. I had to come to term with how things must have been significantly worse. Pro-slavery writers frequently cited higher rates of intellectual disabilities, blindness, and deafness among free Black people in the arctic States to demonstrate how freedom from bondage only increased the need for incapacity. For clinical research, some disabled African American slaves were purchased or hired out. which demonstrates how slaves were expected to perform physically so that potential buyers would not be able to tell that they had any physical disabilities. While not all owners of bondservants treated sick or disabled slaves with care and provided medical attention, many were wary of their slaves' claims of vulnerability or damage. If my ancestors could endure this suffering, so can we. We are not alone, and we have a chance of surviving and thriving. People with disabilities and those without disabilities both experience problems.

Turner, "African American Slavery and Disability: Bodies, Property, and Power in the Antebellum South, African American Slavery and Disability: Bodies, Property, and Power in the Antebellum South, 1800–1860."

Donating to charity is for those who have it to give. I will not preach to you that if you come to Jesus all your problems are behind you and you are going to end up immeasurably blessed. it is common knowledge however that it requires a massive amount of confidence boldness and faith, regardless of your faith, to reach new heights. if you have a mental barrier and fear of heights and fixated on being destitute and staying stuck, you can forget about it. There are a multitude of people who bash prosperity preachers, I am not going to judge all prosperity preachers and I get that we live in a society that appoints judges so I get that at times we must be judgmental, and the bible speaks on poverty, riches, judging and not.

The majority of the country and world is poor or close to poor, at this point so naturally folks are going to have a lot of harsh feelings when it comes to prosperity preaching, there is also coveting occurring even though of course God wants all of us to prosper. On the off chance that I as a destitute individual needed to pick between hearing a lesson about how not to get rich versus how to get rich. I would pick the message about getting rich. I do not need to surrender my life to have never-ending life nor do you. Recall out of the multitude of spots God might have put you he set you in a rich nation and was it for mediocrity? C'mon.

Let justice reign

It is exhibited that because both adults with disabilities and those with special needs can compete in the Olympics, both Special Olympics and the Olympics have this in common: if you participate in one or the other, you are still an Olympian. Specialization in one category is common, just as both types of Olympics include a variety of activities.

Employed members of protected groups are entitled to workplace accommodations.

This is good news from a benefit perspective because you can also get SSI or SSDI, a disability attorney from legal aid, take a medical leave of absence from school, and get your money back. Do you know what? Even though having a disability interferes with our daily lives and makes it difficult for us to show others the strong and healthy side of ourselves,

We can still be strong despite the illnesses and challenges we encounter.

People occasionally mistake our disability for a flaw when it is a mental illness or general disability and there is a distinction, especially when it is a significant part of who we are and causes us to experience constant disruption. A further benefit is belonging to a trustworthy neighborhood.

See part of the invisible advantage of being an adult with special needs is being excellent at seeing the world in extraordinary ways, having the skill to not be absurd, and having a knack for talking about it as it is. We do not want to profess to intrigue you, and we are not exactly obsessed with continuously letting you know what you need to hear. We do not want to profess to intrigue you, and we are not exactly wild about continuously letting you know what you need to hear. making a typical showing is the number of honeyed words you possess to be to have the honor of staying in diverse subjection. my previous boss once consented to death, which I declined even though my previous colleague called our workplace a manor.

If you are fortunate, you should live on tipping in what should be the zenith of working life. You can live on tips and the world will ensure you get the lowest pay permitted by law on the grounds that the world makes bogus commitments about ensured tips. At Wholefoods we likewise got tips and they were consistently irregular. I prescribe restricting yourself to occupations that have an explanation that does not have anything to do with you, however, should be a continuous issue that you need to acknowledge eventually.

Clearly there are a ton of convincing opportunists out there seeking to seize upon misleading us so we must stay on guard. if you desire to prepare an LLC, you can simply comprise your LLC out of state the consequence might not be as simple. If I did so in my domestic kingdom of New Jersey, however, it would nonetheless be difficult due to double taxation because my LLC would face judgement as each a home and an overseas organization. I at the start had a goal date in idea for when I desired to begin a business, however after cautious consideration, I determined it would be tons greater recommended to write a e book like this first for the established public. This explains why I have been getting to know proudly owning an LLC a good deal and why I am insightful about it barring having to take any classes. If you determine to go to one of these web sites to buy a bundle for the formation of your LLC, you must preserve in thinking that you want to behavior lookup first if you do not favor to go through whilst a commercial enterprise grows.

African Americans draft authorities In 1983, the law also included a provision that allowed wealthy men to pay $300 to avoid the draft; consequently, in New York City, dissenters drove four days of horrific assaults against African American draft authorities loaded fiscal specialists and protestant ministers in 1983, the high court overturned the conviction of Raymond Dirks, an enterprise master who communicated private data to his guests and This case exemplifies middle-class flightiness during the administrations of the liberal master equity duke maze and the moderate equity duke maze in the 1960s.

Antonin Scalia voted for representatives in the 7 percentile of non-middle-class felonies and the 82 percentile of middle-class crimes. However, the courts' passions have been the discourse on an endless series of licit training that has extended the freedoms of well-off people and associations, going from the boons of government backing successors to one side to named counsel in felonious cases for more than 50 times. During Nixon's political campaign in 1968, he promised to end the indigent people who cherished the maze court and replace it with a perfectionist court. Rich youths or possibly kids in richer areas were one of the main gatherings the new safe court saved. There was a developing agreement among lower regulatory courts, state courts, and regulation preceptors that the original security condition anticipated countries to indeed outspend poor and unfortunate academy areas in 1973, yet the court, by a 5-to-4 vote, pronounced that Texas and other countries reserved the option to spend additional cash on kids in richer regions.

Cohen, "How the Supreme Court Favors the Rich and Powerful."

"A New York Rioter Explains His Opposition to the Draft · SHEC: Resources for Teachers."

In 2022, New York chooses to pay opulent landowners to accept rent vouchers. "The goal for the Democrats is to make section 8 housing everywhere," one commenter wrote. That is false, I say as a poor disabled woman, and others agree. Bipartisanship boosts self-esteem.

Many people associate the term "public benefits" with cash distributed to the poor, but this is not the case. Middle-class people are among those who receive benefits from the nation's major social insurance programs, such as Social Security, Medicare, and unemployment insurance.

All out misperceptions about who gets public advantages and for what intentions are driving the country toward discusses that divert from the genuine issues confronting working class and low-pay Americans.

36% of nuclear families have a matured or crippled type. With regards to Medicaid, in 2008, 65% of costs were for those 65+, visually impaired, or crippled.

reality:

Most Americans tolerate prepaid utilities

reality:

Most Open Benefits Aimed at Low-Wage Americans Don't Take Cash

reality:

Consistently low interest in bundles to help Americans in need

reality:

Low-wage beneficiaries are often elderly or disabled

reality:

Interest in programs to help Americans in need is low

Use on educational cost, preparing, work, and social administrations has been a reliably little piece of the complete government financial plan, around 3%. Altogether, spending on these projects in monetary 2011, which completed in late Sep., may have put him simply more than $120 gazillion. On the other hand, security spending is in excess of multiple times higher, at an expected $768 billion for the 2011 monetary year.

The deciding component: Moderate manner of speaking that the central government regularly gives out checks to individuals who are excessively lethargic to work is inadmissibly incorrect.

"The Facts About Americans Who Receive Public Benefits."

Employees

After buying a Groupon to save money and being told my order was cancelled by the Domino's worker that does not know about how that works and that they do not participate in a third-party vendor offering. I could not even get his name. Groupon ended up giving me store credit. So many stores are like that, nostalgically working at Whole Foods and finding a leaked video from Amazon related to unions and Amazon and Whole Foods are not the same company but Amazon is a backer for Whole Foods, I ended up sharing it with a coworker we both ended up quitting. The funny thing is she ended up going to work for Amazon after that, but she remembered that video and she wanted to do it for an abbreviated time for the pay or as, so we say.

Since checking out that training video obviously intended for management leaked out by a group that wants unionization, I also found all the alleged negatives that were brought up didn't seem so negative to a negative person like me. One of my supervisors at Whole Foods sounded familiarized with the same script and he ended up telling me how unions don't do anything and how It disrupts the flow between the managers and the workers, I have a news for you, you're all employees it's just that a lot of managers act like owners of the company because that is the incentive, and which is why it's confusing at times.

A minority of specialists quit their jobs in mild protest of their bosses' involvement in their unhatched pay. The bosses, on the other hand, have a great hobby at work and fire their employees for no reason, clarification, or notice. Achievement requires security, fortitude, and certainty. After some time, free settlements became less well known. I understand that there are people who have little financial means and are aware of their limitations, but they agree to do similar work until the end of their lives. Notwithstanding, if describes you, read on for some alternatives. Over time, free exchange has become commonplace. I understand that there are people who have little control over their finances and are unable to determine their limits, yet they are determined to work in similar occupations until the end of their lives. In any case, if this happens as frequently as possible, search for certain choices.

A few selections may have stricter requirements than unique, unbiased undertakings. Managers and employees covered by joint log-moving agreements may have the option to reach edges that are no longer reachable via cost assortment. A partner's certificates chief will not be jobless in the tournament if each of the pioneers and the hand have an exaggerated understanding. Bosses cannot terminate representatives for abusing the authorities' rules. Laborers suddenly change occupations. A fourteen-day observer period is typically prescribed for her to maintain a decent standing with probable businesses. Would you like to be fashionable to be in the most diverse social class, or the least wealthy? It finally depends on you. Regardless, consider one situation. So, assuming your occupation is unstable to such an extent that you quit in less than fourteen days, determine how you will respond when you return. Does free commercial enterprise imply you are going off course without exhortation? quick and painless. Still, it is hip to claim to get red lingerie at any point soon. Is it true that you are a challenge seeker looking for an undertaking at some point during a period of popularity? If this is true, you qualify for an information exchange reward. Could it happen at some point? Given the circumstances, there is nothing greater to it.

Doyle, "What Is a Sign-on Bonus?"

Doyle, "What Does Employment At-Will Mean?"

If someone decides that they are going to just keep on taking low paying jobs that do not pay a living wage that person might as well be free to work at a job that is their dream job because they are following their heart even though they are not using their head. the problem is too many people will keep dealing with toll hikes and train fare hikes and they don't want to let their team down and they'll take an intermittent leave of absence, and they'll do everything to avoid leaving because they know that they're not going to get unemployment or severance pay if they decide to walk away. when you are in that situation you have already overextended yourself overstayed your welcome and have no choice but to leave. the unemployment agency is always looking for a way to avoid paying which I understand. I have looked at a letter that has stated that I didn't have to leave my job despite having a meltdown on the sales floor from the stress of having to be so independent while on a team.

I recall when my former team leader said that no matter how others make it seem and they will make it seem like it that they'll be fine without me and that I should take a leave of absence if I need to because when the company is ready to fire me they'll fire me and I remember how an assistant team leader over her said that employees are babies and that you have to treat them like you would one of your children. what is it going to take? before numerous people say I am an adult I will be heard, and I will be seen, and I am not putting up with this anymore.

As opposed to squandering excessive time at the store.

Shopping malls dominate America's optional schools.

U. S. In comparison to education, residents spend $100 billion more on watches, diamonds, and shoes.

The next time someone tries to convince you of the value of higher education, if it is not too much trouble, let them know about my book.

In America, there are more shopping malls than secondary schools.

To cause a stir in the community while delivering the least amount, 50% of virtual customers will increase the size of their orders. Approximately 2/3 of the U.S. S. Exchange utilization produces GDP (gross domestic product).

Stop wasting time on shoddy work; it is so bad that it's estimated that the average person will spend 33 percent of their life working. Over your lifetime, which equates to about 90,000 hours of work. Stop wasting time at gatherings and attending pointless events; start directing them thoroughly.

Even though gatherings are not always a huge waste of time, research has shown that they are not always beneficial either. The following astounding findings about gatherings came from an Atlassian-directed review: 91% of employees dream of getting together. 39 percent of representatives have dozed off during meetings.

96% of people have missed something, such as a scheduled event.

While at a gathering, 73% of attendees were preoccupied with something else.

Representatives in the majority think meetings are useless.

89 percent of representatives complain about pointless or difficult meetings.

Given that you understand the point and I do not want to elaborate, I'll stop here. This must stop immediately.

Given that you understand the point and I don't want to elaborate, I'll stop here. This has to stop immediately.

"15 Employee Productivity Statistics You Want to Know (2022)."
Becker, "17 Staggering Statistics About Our Shopping Habits."
"Becoming Minimalist."
"How Many Hours Does the Average Person Work Per Week?"

If you need balance, then make a balance sheet and separate your debt into two special columns so that the accurate debt, such as student loans for technical education, etc., and enterprise loans, can go on your left and the terrible debt, such as credit cards and other revolving debt loans for cars and payday loans, can go on the proper side.

You can use a savings card to make an ill-advised purchase and still avoid going into debt if you use it correctly and it increases your arbitrary net worth. Even so, it is extremely dangerous, and you do not want to have to restart. You need to purchase what you can manage to pay for and learn to go without.

Just keep getting extra cash and do not rack up debt, knowing you cannot pay it back under any circumstances. A scholar loan is another traditional instance of healthy debt that can turn out to be bad for one's financial fitness above a positive level. Sure, it is funding for your education and therefore the possibility of greater lifetime earnings. But numerous studies point to student debt as an important reason millennials may additionally delay shopping for a home, saving for retirement, or working towards other long-term financial goals. The only guarantee with university is that you will graduate with a degree; employers simply choose to understand when they hire a vet or a university graduate that they have been mentally conditioned for being an excellent employee and will provide up riches for minor incentives that the worker cannot precisely appraise but has staying power.

"Personal Finance Education | TD Ameritrade."

This will be entertaining. Are you still unsure? This should assist.

Not everyone is fit for a supervisory job. There are lots of reasons why teams opt out of managerial positions.

Me: Right, some people should be promoted to C.E.O. in another company.

You do not need to be a principal to make more money.

Me: That is true; you can boost your earnings the most by not working for anybody else at all.

Trace your rewards so you can impart them to present and future employers.

Yes, I was told to do that once; it does not matter when the company is literally falling apart, and things are so bad that stations must be shut down to keep up.

1. Address Individuals

Be open about your chosen career path. Start with the interview method: ask about professional growth at the company as well as the path of the person who formerly held the position for which you are interviewing.

Instead, you can tell your boss directly once you are engaged and open a conversation about how to grow your career without stepping into management.

2. View for Flat Pyramids

Some firms have a "move up or move out" kind of attitude; if personnel are not being promoted to higher-level positions, the company assumes that the employee must not be a good fit.

3. Think about contracts.

Working as a service provider can also be a way to avoid administration.

4. Work at a start-up or small-scale company.

Occasionally, inaugurations and reduced companies put together small organizations and personnel with big titles.

5. Say no Don't tolerate taking on tasks that involve manual management.

Burry, "How to Make More Money If You Don't Want to Be a manager."

Here is something to think about: how would you like to be another statistic? Try not to be the person who has not been fired thus far. Thus far, forty people have been discharged from a task in their career, firing a representative that will be swapped out. Charges range between 161 and 201 percent of their yearly wage, increasing as high as 213 for high-ranking officials. How often do people lose their job?

Six million people lose their jobs each month, or seventy-two million per year, or about 45 percent of the workforce. Of course, many people lose or leave their jobs more than once, so the total number of people changing jobs is significantly less than seventy-two million, and more than forty-five million people enter or re-enter the labor force each month. poor work efficiency This is the most quoted excuse for a deal.

Termination misbehavior: some types of misconduct can not only lead to your termination but can also have legal costs. Chronic tardiness avoids being 30 minutes late; approximately twenty-two of our employers' fired employees for a phony sick call; violations of company policy and regulations led to it; their violation led to job loss; using drugs or alcohol at work; approximately seventy of the 148 million people who abuse drugs work; personal use of company property. Regular use of everything from copiers to printers for your side business can lead to job loss. theft or damage to property: taking anything, including your company's pen or paper, for personal use is not only an offense of arson, but it can also lead to legal problems. fake company report improper use of social media, insubordination.

Baker, "Six Million People Lose or Leave Their Job Every Month (That's 72 million a Year for Arithmetic Fans) - Center for Economic and Policy Research."

"The Top 10 Reasons People Get Fired - Perkins Asbill, A Professional Corporation."

Whether you are going to remain an employee or going to become an employer, you need to gain Insight so that you can have a better perspective when it comes to seeing the correlation between how we all are already in situations that are financially risky and that being an entrepreneur is just another essential risk taken on in capitalism. We also need to know how this affects us personally.

en·tre·pre·neur

noun: entrepreneur; plural noun: entrepreneurs

a person who assembles and runs a business or companies, taking on larger than normal monetary risks as they must.

a promoter within the entertainment industry.

We can see that putting ourselves out there is just as important as being willing to take on the rest in business.

There are many ways to classify a company's financial risk. One approach to this is to classify financial risks into four broad categories.

Market threat, credit risk, liquidity risk, operational danger. Bonus: Currency risk is the risk of adverse exchange rate fluctuations between the operating and trading currencies. Companies that diversify into foreign markets or rely heavily on imports and exports of goods are most at risk. 1. identify risks 2. Assess and document risks 3. Delegation of administrative procedures4. Act 5. Monitor/Maintain Progress

Conclusion Implementing a financial risk assessment process in your organization will help your finance team better understand the potential risks to all business decisions.

Maverick, "What Are the Major Categories of Financial Risk for a Company?"

"5 Things to Include in Your Financial Risk Assessment Process."

"Definition of ENTREPRENEUR."

"What Is Financial Risk & How to Assess It | Allianz Trade In USA."

Consider taking a job that has staffing problems. For example, a plumber or an electrician.

The more skills you understand from a particular profession, the more you can get a job and earn more money, so ideally you can enjoy your job or retire before owning property. Becoming a proprietor, flipping a house, or starting to sell money associated with one's own home and proudly owning a home is an added threat to buying a home given the threat of combat., perfect for renting where it only takes a month. It may take years for you to be kicked out. Time is cash, and owning a home lets you have more time to get everything straightened out, much like a savings card gives you more time to pay than a debit card. Matters are perpetually confusing, but if you give yourself an edge, adjust your monthly payments, and maintain your home, you will become richer. Working your brain as a side hustle behind your job, or ideally as a full-time sole proprietorship, will set you apart and set you on the path to success. B. Use networking like an investor with an anonymous investor, sponsor, or co-founder, or in business activities at meetups, or attend free real estate seminars on YouTube.

Please accept it.

Being a PC hacker or marijuana extractor is also a high paying job.
Value is set in ways such as facilities, demand, and rarity.

Birt, "15 Odd Jobs That Pay Well."

I do not mean this judgmentally; I mean it instructionally. Are you reasonable enough to comprehend that our savings function without any commotion? One of the ruling classes stands out because it is quiet but fashionable. I will present you a hint: it's horrible. I notice that the initial dents are designed to be optimal. Which financial structure do you judge to be ideal? It will close to certainly be the person we have immediately assigned to you.

The extent of trade, known as macroeconomics, is investigated by means of how savings run and function. Microeconomics is the arm of commerce that studies by what method inhabitants' offspring and arrangements create economic determinations; it is the contrast of macroeconomics. Micro-monetary schemes are distinct types of large-scale monetary structures.

It is a branch of business that studies the finances and administrative patterns of individuals, households, and societies. Monetarism is a macroeconomic plan that contends that governments can claim business-related security as well as the ability to supply various important laws by focusing on the advancement price of the coins. Keynesian trade resold by statisticians' bathrooms Maynard Keynes This macroeconomic law is unquestionably part of the administration's plan to stabilize the finances. The spirit in the following commercialism is novelty finance and markets, allowing traders and contractors to trade their taxes; basically, they envision guardianship and produce that supply that returns to humans, accompanying more charge assortment buyers and causing bureaucracy to be free to the population, which necessitates more capital borrowers. The mammoth stock market The NYSE constantly trades trillions of dollars, accompanying the use and sale of stocks by publicly traded companies.

A search display is primarily a sustained decrease in advantage charges. A used-up advertisement occurs concurrently with an activity. Big advertiser indications are down by a factor of twenty from their current peak. A rising market is technically concurrent with an activity, and the stock exchange sees a progress of twenty from allure to premature reduction of a component. A search in retail is the antithesis, with dips accompanying the source of the use of "oodles." On search, people are for sale.

No nonsense, as remarkable people anticipate, when will the work and result control of the United States of America accompany the ability of non-public landowners to use for gain in proximity to support the use of the United States of America?

Marxism is a set of publics, governmental, and business-related principles chosen later. Karl Marx's book discusses the impact of a loose manufacturer on difficult labor output as well as profession and association incidents, and it advocates for an employee coup to invalidate commercialism down to and through socialism. The price stretchiness of the decision for a few elements is -2 a 10 tumor in value, which causes the decision for quotas to fall alongside the capability of the use of twenty inflexible event supplies or name for a few acts is numb to vacillations in any other changeable containing price.

The time-ending stiffness, referred to as a portion, means that a widowed profession in charge of an amazing or wage earner does not immediately have any more capacity to meet an eligible supply with merchandise in the amount required for specific merchandise, and skilled workers have no extra demand because the increase in giving has no link.

Because skilled labor is no longer in demand, the individual percent supply burst no longer has a reward.

The output gap shows that the savings' peak profit is beneath the allure of maximum volume. When harvest exceeds ability, swelling increases; when output falls below volume, swelling decreases. Divide the GDP breach in each real view by the ability GDP, a suggestion of correction GDP, and multiply by 100 to calculate the GDP breach.

(Output gap wallsteetmojo.com) "20 Basic Terms Used in Economics."

Keep in mind a solitary penny; Others need their whole money supplanted. Have you known about US government dollarization? I positively do not. We should likewise focus on expansion and retirement, gives that worry us all. At the point when you comprehend the significance of your cash, your ways of managing money will become perfect.

Dollarization

at the point when a nation's own money in the host nation is supplanted by the US dollar as the residents' favored cash. This could be the aftereffect of intentional government strategies or some singular trading choices (for example Latin American financial backers frequently forsake the dollar at the earliest hint of concern) With regards to government strategy, dollarization is an intense money related commission.
Watch out, would we say we are tricked? This is another uncommon word. disinflation Lower expansion. This implies that the cost will dial back yet not fall. This is called collapse. Because of changes in the worldwide economy and a more extended future, many individuals in the world are compelled to work better compared to their fanciful age because of an absence of stores. Contingent upon the country you live in, there are different annuity and advantage plans accessible to residents. The UK, Republic of Singapore, Malaysia, USA, Australia, and Canada all have altogether separate ways to deal with guaranteeing their residents have good retirement pay. A few nations, for example, the Unified Realm, set a compulsory retirement age, while others, for example, Singapore, offer re-business programs for resigned laborers to give more open doors. The affiliation provides food more towards the old.

Economics A-Z terms beginning with D | The Economist

Moran, "Retirement Plans from Around the World."

Them: This advice has been given to you before, yet it could be the most crucial for preventing overspending. The chance of making expensive impulse purchases is eliminated if you never carry credit cards with you. Consider carrying cash most of the time and only the amount you can afford to spend, even though it may sound a little retro. Only bring the plastic if you are certain, you will need it.

Me: This relates to being an indebted shopaholic; what I am talking about is being set apart. You can do this until you can do better since you need eternal self-control, so life is not out of control.

Them: Try engaging in the following brief mental exercise the next time you go shopping: Place an item in your cart that you want but do not actually need and leave it there so you can view it the entire time. It will start to feel like yours after a while.

Me: We do not even need to go any further; we can see how delirious this becomes.

Them: Ask your spouse, brother, sister, or a friend who is familiar with you before spending, say, $4,000 on a high-end 24-horsepower lawn tractor. You might decide after some debate that the $1,200, 14-horsepower job will suffice.

Me: To be fair, I wanted to prove how absurd this article gradually became. I am by no means encouraging bad behavior; I'm encouraging you to keep it that way and splurge as needed, selectively.

Small splurges are better than big ones from a personal finance standpoint because they are less expensive.

Me: There is our common ground.

Them: "Hide" Money in a Tax-Sheltered Account

Me: Or seek help—a 401(k) or an IRA is not mental health care.

"5 Easy Ways to Fight the Urge to Splurge."

We have witnessed it, or I think we have experienced it. Did you know that there is an effortless way to avoid constant interruptions at work? Layoffs continue unless the workplace imposes quotas or deadlines and prohibits general work stoppages. I have worked at jobs and irregular companies in many places, but I have never seen it the other way around. Every three minutes and five seconds, the staff takes a break to catch up with the UC Irvine researchers. This means that for every 26 minutes a worker spends at work, they can dedicate 3 minutes of labor.

Let us use the word right here. Let me introduce you to the term self-employment, but procrastination often leads to running out of money. Equality is relevant if you work as a worker. They pay you until they cannot pay you anymore, after which they fire you. Despite the fact that going out of business often results in zero cash flow, I use the unmarried term for sole proprietorship.

They will pay you compensation until you can catch up with the enterprise while you are gone. You can change the way you get paid while you are self-employed. 86% of people can replace a picture with their own picture. Whether working from home or an office, more than 86% of employees would like to paint themselves. According to staff, there are fewer distractions while being able to isolate oneself from others. Plus, they are fully aware of their work because they do not have to act or communicate in a positive way. This autonomy is further extended to missions. Instead of leaving the shared task to others, many employees can paint alone. Workers must complete more complex courses in self-employment, but this is the case in most cases. Now that we have witnessed it or mastered it on our part, here is the correct model. Did you already know that there is a fantastic way to avoid having to stop the facts in your work? Additionally, layoffs continue while offices set quotas or deadlines and prohibit extended holidays. I worked in unusual local workshops and temporary organizations, but I did not perceive it differently. According to UC Irvine consultants, every 3 minutes, five erratic employees get interrupted. This means that for every 26 minutes a worker spends at work, they can perform a total of 3 minutes of work. Let me say something here.

Catmull, "How to Manage Your Cash Flow as a Solo Entrepreneur."

"Merriam Webster."

We can hear and see a bunch of European Americans constantly ignorantly insisting that Black people should not mind when others call us the N word since we call ourselves N*ggas in Rap and Hip Hop. Hip Hops cultural roots stem from African American people who faced discrimination in other industries and had to sell out to get ahead and the same thing is happening today just like when you are at work and cannot be yourself. Whites are still the majority domestically even if they identify otherwise, and accountants and lawyers run the music industry. I never hear anybody tell a gay person that they cannot call themselves a gay slur and if they do then the rest of us must. Being Homosexual and being African is not one in the same you wouldn't know as such judging by how interracial marriage and same sex marriage keeps being mashed up due to discrimination and the legal premise of gay marriage. Jonny McGovern's song Lookin' Cute feelin' Cute and includes blaspheme and has F*g in it that does not mean I have to favor it and identify as a Hag Stag so I can sing it to Lesbigay people, which is obviously a double standard. When we say the word N*gger it makes us feel uncomfortable as is because it is meant to, and those of you know that and still want to use it but if you are repeating it to educate that is at minimum superior.

Decisions and directions

While less fortunate I choose to pay my academy dues in coins. I took the blue box to the counselor's office. The coins I handed over were declined by a consultant who told me I could keep them and that the charges would be deducted anyway. sometimes we just need to get creative and decide to pay certain bills in an unusual but respectable way. My advisor was had the choice whether to accept them or not.

It works on the outside, but what about the inside? if you need a product that is overpriced and fragile, check the inside once it breaks. You will know what cheap effects you're buying, and you'll be able to say if you'd use the savings equivalent or think about time-matching the prices and why you wouldn't mentally lower the price in the malignant price label because you've previously decided. why do you mentally lower the price? despite When I went shopping for glasses, the salesman tried to convince me that I might not break them if I spent the extra plutocrat on them, even though he did the job, you know why I left without the specs I planned to buy for the erector - by force. Also, when cyber patrons keep supporting a seller who has a well-known sales coaching company and has already shown that he has his superior content online for free and doesn't have the same quality on paid content and stretches it out constantly, at one point, he even offered work and didn't mind if someone had to take out a loan to pay for it while a worker recommended it. Others should worry about the free shirt displayed from a prior customer.

There are distinct kinds of marriages such as arranged marriages and there are also marriages that bloom from an introduction from a mutual friend. Just in case you are getting married, or you know someone that is getting married, it is important to bring up what engaged couples should be discussing beforehand. now by all means I am in favor of premarital counseling, I am also in favor of couples counseling. I think that it does not always have to be a situation where you wait until it is so severe or too late. Ideally a couple at the very least will be willing to keep the lines of communication open and ensure they are compatible. Prenuptial agreement or postnuptial, economic objectives, debt, how bills are going be paid, measuring risk aversion, addressing money being comingled, draw conclusion on how many children you both are going to have, consider getting physical exams, aside from finances discussing which role the in-laws will play and how intimacy is going to work, you need to be aware of each other's libido and limitations. Figure out how the chores are going to be completed.

Monitor the contrast between your version of being wed and theirs and see how much it aligns. considering how the definition of marriage legally has drastically shifted and how society has a different vantage point of what marriage looks like or the possible image of it even if certain individuals do not think it should be a certain way due to their own religious convictions or how they had been raised.

Ignoring the process of how we oversee remains will do us no good, the surviving family members should be able to weigh their needs and the dying person's last wish against the realities of their situation, regardless of whether people choose burning or entombment. Cremation would be a practical choice if budgetary constraints are a significant factor. The traditional burial method is preferable, especially if the deceased was a Christian and if the family has no financial difficulties. Who are we kidding? If we do not have life insurance or make funeral arrangements in advance, all people will be thinking about when we pass away is the cost, which will exacerbate the grief and overshadow our death.

Death leaves us grieving, we all face eternal life, and tragedy is always grave. While the average national funeral, including burial and viewing, costs $7,650, the median funeral costs fall by over $9,000 through the vault. However, because many funeral homes may choose to handle the cremation themselves, the average cost is only about $350. The four fundamental types of life insurance policies' average monthly costs are as follows: $52 per month for whole life insurance. monthly payment of $55 for universal life insurance. The monthly premium for variable life insurance is $40. Cost of term life insurance per month: $53.

Bond, "Average Life Insurance Cost in 2021."

"Burial And Cremation, What Are Their Pros and Cons? - Tranquility Funeral Services."

Examine the man's character and your circumstances in advance to determine whether he's the kind of man who would be willing to cooperate in any way with respects to revocation. Putting dogma away, another important factor to take into account is the cost of revocations. I realize this is a sensitive content and that there are numerous different reasons why women choose to have revocations. likewise, I'm apprehensive that politics need not be fitted into the discussion of revocation because reality prevails. The median cost of having a baby with health insurance is $,000 and$ 854; birth control costs between$ 0 and$ 50 per month; and the same source estimates that a revocation will bring between$ 568 and$ 775.

As the saying goes, a woman's body is her own choice, and she alone will be responsible for taking care of any health issues performing from the revocation. With this in mind, you should seriously consider whether a woman has a revocation through drug or surgery. You have the same freedom to exercise whatever you want and to pierce free birth control, too. The cost of surgery increases as you progress. Just as if you had kept the baby grounded on his passions, you would be completely responsible for the revocation's cost. Being a better diary, including family planning, will raise your tone- worth. Consider getting legal counsel to learn about the revocation laws in your state before traveling to get one. attorneys who bestow to answer questions online through the American Bar Association give free, nonpublic legal advice. Budget for all implicit costs associated with the trip if you choose to travel for a revocation. You should budget for similar particulars as lodging, gas, food, childcare, pet sitting, time off from work, and machine or aeroplane tickets.

Smith, “How Much Does an Abortion Cost? - NerdWallet.”

Rivelli, “How Much Does It Cost to Have a Baby? 2022 Averages.”

You should be litigious whenever you have a viable case and the opportunity to sue. In fact, I am currently receiving settlement funds from a workman's compensation case. The fact that this has to do with principles and financial intelligence is something that the average person misses. Because you sue for everything from loss of affection to medical malpractice, you are not being a vexatious litigant. Even a divorce is a legal proceeding. It is unnecessary for other people to exaggerate; it cannot continue. Nobody understands the emotional or physical suffering you are going through, and even lawyers who have nothing to do with your case should not use their legal knowledge to discourage people from filing lawsuits. Simply unwind, concentrate on both yourself and your attorney, and ensure that your lawyer does a respectable job.

The average payout is low due to the high number of class-action lawsuits.

Even if it only costs $50 for one person, the deal is still worthwhile. The amount of money awarded in these lawsuits can reach the billions of dollars, and the typical settlement can cover hundreds of thousands of people. The amount of compensation received by the plaintiffs determines the scope of a class-action lawsuit.

A fee arrangement may be reached with an attorney. Some may charge a variable contingent fee based on how long the case takes to complete. If the case settles, the attorney may charge a 25% contingency fee; if the case goes to trial, a 30% contingency fee; or higher percentages if the case is appealed. An award-based variable fee may be offered by others: 30% of the initial $100,000, 25% of the subsequent $100,000, and so on.

"Average Class Action Lawsuit Payout in 2019 - Times Laws."

A spendthrift is the polar opposite of a thrifty person, where thrifty means frugal and spendthrift means a big spender. Based on the research, let us assess the assorted reasons why you make the purchases you do. Because I think saving, investing, and spending are important, I fall into both categories. You spend the way you do because your positions, your beliefs, and your desires all influence what you buy.

Your sexual orientation, race, gender, and the religion that shapes your identity can all affect your spending. You are free to pursue your desires, and that is your right. However, keep in mind that only God knows the motivations of manufacturers, who may choose to adopt a business strategy that allows them to easily exploit an LGBTQ identity, racial makeup, religious background, or gender for their own gain and at your expense by following trends and putting their prejudices and differences with you or your population on the back burner. It only takes someone to understand why you buy the things you do and to gain your trust in order for them to take advantage of you when you are in sales, which is why having a high sense of self-worth, avoiding peer pressure when it comes to making purchases, and resisting the strong urge to engage in identity politics are all crucial.

Marriage is the most important investment you will ever make, I have never wed but I know how financially devastating this is, you are paying for a breakup that would have been free if unmarried. With that said marriage is a legally binding contract protect yourself during the lawsuit against the opposing side.

Organize all your paperwork. Immediately terminate joint credit cards and/or other lines of credit. If your spouse refuses to cancel, arrange for your name to be removed from their account. Also, confirm you have a personal bank account.

Choose whether you can remain at the home. It is significant to remember that in terms of custody, the spouse who resides in the home is in a better position.

Get a duplicate of these: Important legal documents such as wills, trusts and marriage contracts

Real Estate Documents Your credit report and credit history, health plan

Receipts for luxuries or major purchases including vehicles and villas.

Joint tax and/or investment accounts. Split and close your account. If the split is an issue, keep the money in an escrow account until the divorce is finalized.

Once you have taken this step, notify your spouse by sending a notarized document.

Important legal documents such as wills, trusts and marriage contracts

Leamon, "How to Protect Yourself in a Divorce | Divorce and Your Money | Avoid Costly Divorce Mistakes."

It is heartbreaking how many of you still see tattoo removal products and tobacco cessation products while never once considering how many people might later regret making similar financial decisions.

"I am the Lord; you shall not cut anything in your flesh for the dead, nor tattoo anything on you. Leviticus 19:28.

Like using savings equivalents as a reward for saving, addiction is the antithesis of freedom. If you let it, the world will transform you into someone entirely different while telling you that you are being accepted and that you are being true to yourself. But what if all you want is to fit in with the rest of the world?

A pastor who wants to live a morally upright life should avoid wasting money on appearance. It is inappropriate and worrying that an unset amount of you would prioritize getting a tattoo overpaying your rent. How can we assume that God is wrong, and we are superior to God if we were not born this way, that way, or a third way? I am positive of this. If you are still having trouble deciding, keep in mind something a counselor once said to me: We can rationalize anything. I am only watching you because I do not want you to make a hasty decision and then regret wasting your money. Everyone, including you and I, is capable.

"Bible Hub."

OSHA estimates that 315 workers per 100,000 per year pass away on the job. If you are a woman, you have close to the same chance of being shot to death or passing away from cervical cancer. Your chances of surviving a workday are higher if your profession is not listed on OSHA.

Which is more deserving of your gratitude: having a job or being alive?

Let's show respect for those who lost their lives while working.

NASA astronaut and physicist Ronald Erwin McNair passed away on January 28, 1986.

He passed away during the launch of the Challenger rocket for STS-51-L.

Stephen Robert Irwin, a zookeeper, conservationist, TV host, wildlife authority, and environmentalist (February 22, 1962–September 4, 2006), was also a proponent of many causes. While he was filming, a short-tailed stingray impaled him in the chest, killing him. The chest wall was deeply damaged by the stingray's penetration.

Christina Victoria Grimmie (March 12, 1994–June 10, 2016) singer, YouTuber, actress, obsessed fan who bought his gun According to the police, he wanted her but couldn't have her, so he killed her; he shot her during the autograph signing after her performance.

South African singer, songwriter, actress, and civil rights activist Zenzile Miriam Makeba was born on March 4, 1932, and died on November 9, 2008.

Makeba got sick while performing on November 9, 2008, in Castel Volturno, an Italian town close to Caserta. She had a heart attack and passed away as a result.

R.I.P. To those who have passed away, please accept my condolences, particularly regarding those who were close to them. Visit http://www.deadorkicking.com to verify if a celebrity is dead.

"Ronald McNair - Wikipedia."

"Steve Irwin - Wikipedia."

"Christina Grimmie - Wikipedia."

"Miriam Makeba - Wikipedia."

"Most Dangerous Jobs in America."

Copeland and Donofrio, "Most Dangerous Jobs in America."

Dunning Kruger's effect pertains to people with a meager skill set, specialties, and history regarding a particular task or area of information who have a psychological bias assuming an increased ability or astuteness. An atheist accused me of that being that I'm a Christian. I think the word the skeptic was searching for is grandiose since it'd be more suitable. I'm a former atheist and have nothing against atheists. We all have a right to refuse to accept God and call it unbelief. Obviously, God's existence doesn't hinge on our acceptance, nor does he care, only man cares.

Akin to how you don't have to accept that this is an economics title, fine, then since in psychology we get to shape our own reality, you're right because of our emotional need, so we cancel each other out. Doubtful people tend to doubt, and their predisposition through intelligent design leads them to resort to worshipping particular scientists who support the propaganda, locking them in an echo chamber and demonizing the rest of the world, and through a preconceived notion of intelligent design, classifying it as pseudoscience. Then getting down to why free thinkers and the financially free aren't using free speech to mention MK Ultra, an illicit, widespread brainwashing study comprising at times unsuspecting citizens using drugs for mental torture and collecting intel for 20 years infiltrated by the CIA who spent at least 10 million. Instead of worrying about "nothing," each creation has a creator, and I hope if nothing else my book doesn't lose faith in me.

Outer stimuli

People should stop using the following statements as excuses to not get themselves out of poverty and out of the middle class and to gain prosperity. These types of cliches and sayings are so banal. I guarantee you that poverty is a problem and causes more problems, whereas riches fix financial problems and help others. Since the majority cannot see themselves there or want to get all the money without taking any necessary steps to get there, they feel the need to self-soothe and spread their propaganda. Do not fall for it if you get rich and realize it is not for you; you are still better off than someone who never even bothered and those who, worst of all, choose to die in their poverty. Explain how someone can migrate to America as an adult with little money and get rich fast, while others were born here and continue to be poorer through various stages. We should not be jealous, but we should wonder because something is not right. Money does not buy happiness.

There are rich people who still are not happy. Money is not everything. I do not care about money. Rich people have gotten rich through corruption. There is more to life than money. I am spiritually rich. Rich people are crazy. Let us stop talking about money. Talking about money makes me mad because I do not have any. Investing is a gamble. You must be lucky to get rich. Plus, stop cherry-picking the Bible to wage a campaign against wealth. Wow, no wonder so many people can barely survive, and plenty more are not thriving. One also should not admire or befriend those who keep saying these regardless of their intent, and since it is common knowledge that you make close to whatever those nearest you make percentage or dollarwise, that alone should give you pause. The problem is that no matter how beneficial we pretend they are, they only exacerbate societal problems.

Many people do not take risks, as is clear in risk avoidance animations. If you love playing, there are financial literacy games available for free, some for adults. I will give you a link so you can find it yourself. No matter how young the game is, relax and enjoy and gain knowledge of all the mature traits. Monopoly is just one aspect of his financial literacy. There is a game called Spent that uses strategic empathy to educate about poverty, also through charities. Instead of upselling you, I am offering this to you free.

Monopoly is only one aspect of financial literacy. There is a game known as "Spent" that employs tactical empathy to educate on poverty, and through a charity. There is a game called "financial football" by Visa. Financial professor Dr. Boyce Watkins has a free podcast, and the public app has a digital community for retail investors.

https://www.stockmarketgame.org/
https://www.creditclash.com/
https://www.mycreditunion.gov/financial-resources/hit-road-financial-adventure
https://buildyourstax.com/
https://senseanddollars.thinkport.org/games/charge/home.html
https://playspent.org/

gamification
[ˌgāməfəˈkāSHən]
NOUN
consist of characteristic elements of game playing (e.g., marking, challenging others, guidelines of play) in other areas of activity, typically as an electronic advertising technique to encourage engagement with a product or service:

There are blank worksheets you can transfer too; would you try it? I recommend you check it all out.

With multiplication, you must think about adding. Flash cards can be useful, as can the multiplication table. You can continually use a calculator, but it just works better for us when we know as much by heart.

Start with smaller numbers, as in "single," then move to bigger numbers; it is easier to multiply 6 x 3 = 18, then 60 x 30 = 1800, even though it is like the first just higher. You want to understand all the basics, from adding and subtracting to multiplying and dividing, since even as adults we do not want to get ahead of ourselves.

"Multiplication Tricks and Tips for Faster Learning"

"22 Financial Literacy Games to Make Learning Fun for Kids, High School Students, and Adults"

There is a lot of materialism and pop subculture that we are both uncovered to thru advertisements, news, or Celebrity gossip on-line and offline. It is going on in the job; it is going on in the store. Without in addition ado, let me current to you all the celebrity-based content that many of you so desperately crave that pertains to finances, and it is going to retailer you time and road default make you money in view that you will have greater time to make cash when you store time.

https://www.wealthygenius.com/hot/

https://www.plungedindebt.com/celebrity-wealth-calculator/

https://www.thethings.com/celebrities-started-own-charities/

Celebrity NFT Owners: Which Celebs Bought NFTs? (business2community.com)

28 Celebrities Who Own Bitcoin (ranker.com)

Top 10: Celebrities who own private jets (Fly Aeolus)

Top 15 Celebrities Who Own Sports Teams (thesportster.com)

Popular searches not listed here: celebrities who possess restaurants; celebrities who possess liquor brands.

I see what many are up to, and while this is incredibly attractive information, y'all need to pay the most interest to how celebs profit and loss, for your personal sake. Your self-worth increases when you can research whilst amused alternatively of dreamy.

Apart from their main profession, this is how they have emerged as so wealthy.

brands, portable apps, royalties, apparel lines, autograph perfumes, and restaurants. Most Jay-Z's fortune stems from investments or groups he launched privately.

"Fashion Lady: Latest Trends and More."

Seeing is believing. Check out the inspiring content and see how far you have come by deciding to receive the blessing God has in store for you. You are getting better. Have fun with yourself and be inspired by what you are moving. others tell you not to worry about achieving your goals What is yours is yours, and you have the same things as others, and you can use those things to get money. Do not worry about being disappointed, expect things to catch you off guard and fail too, but recognize that it doesn't matter because you're still doing what you have to do. Just because there are bumps in the road doesn`t mean you will not get closer. So what? There are potholes on the road. The Vehicle also crashes Airplanes have their problems, but people still get transported. You have met and will meet plenty of people, whom you could not progress with because you did not finish what you set out to do. You will be able to get more financial help because you are now more likely to get help from a supportive group.

You can find all of the following on you YouTube:

1.Actively chase your dreams full episode praise on TBN

https://youtu.be/xg1ccuWs89U

2.Teaching you a rich person's concept multiples of 10

https://youtu.be/RGk8QXVnsN8

3. A frontline documentary

https://youtu.be/2mHsTKvAuZc

4.End of the road how money became worthless, free documentary https://youtu.be/cTMna_vYDJg

5.Train your brain to make more money:

https://youtu.be/BrRZZ_8NTkg

There are undeniably more mini-computers accessible than the sort found on our mobile phones or tip-adding machines. the number of mini-computers that you are acquainted with; I'm finding out about additional mini-computers than at any other time; here are a few number crunchers to assist you with your estimations much faster than a lot of the other methods; you're going to want to pay very close attention to the salary calculator.

https://www.calculator.net/salary-calculator.html

While you're at it, you're going to want to check out this one as well.

https://www.calculatorpro.com/calculator/fuel-consumption-calculator/

Just do yourself a favor and try
them all.

https://captaincalculator.com/financial/economics/

Ah, globalization.

https://www.theglobaleconomy.com/compare-countries/

Compare countries before purchasing your next lottery ticket.
You can find out your odds of winning through calculation.

https://www.calculatorpro.com/calculator/lottery-calculator/

Hopefully the familiar effect with a twist is ensuring you find this a good read.

Since most of us still cannot afford to indulge in an upscale experience as much as we would like, here is an affordable and great substitute. viewing luxury magazines that give us an inside look into what it must be like to be rich without being rich. I just downloaded one now and looking at it is so stunning. They target the affluent, but since that is our target, we should be able to freely read them all the same, right? So, let us do it. As usual, here is a disclaimer: do not end up broke trying to get rich or look rich.

What I want you to do is what you need to do, and that is find some visual way through a magazine or take a walk in a genuinely nice neighborhood to be inspired to be rich. Look, it is either this or you can keep on looking at news coverage of tropical islands and watching commercials for tourist attractions. The closer you get to riches mentally; it is only a matter of time before you have them tangibly.

Here are some to get you started: Afar Magazine Global Living Magazine uptown magazine Haute living Islands magazine Luxury Living magazine Robb report

Empathize or you will covet; they do not cry there, but we know it is a sin.

If you believe this Genesis 1:27 So God created mankind in his own image—in the image of God, he created them. Male and female, he created them.

Prove it: being godlike is not blasphemous.

"Bible Gateway Passage: Genesis 1:27 - Amplified Bible."

I do not forget hearing Elon Musk say that he did not assume Tesla might be triumphant because it was a vehicle company. Which kind of enterprise do you think it is?

In step with Kevin O'Leary's son, who says it is a data company, the point is that you recognize the call and the face, and if you do not, you need to ask a person. Be cautious about that choice, though, factually like how Elon Musk desired Twitter and it was losing money, you should make sure that what you are needing is going to have an exceptionally good payoff. You continually study the figures and use them to parent it out. When you observe these kinds of people and you see them going to work even as the entirety of their lives is going wrong and no longer working out for them, and they have prioritized their activity over themselves, you must ask yourself, "Who do they have to blame?" On the last day that I labored at my previous job, they wanted me to be a janitor, and they wanted to ensure that I would be a cashier assistant too, which I did, and then I left. Guess what happened after? It transformed me, just as it did or would.

Listen to music that will end up reminding you of the consequences of not getting rich and influence you to get rich: I just got paid by Johnny Kemp and covered by NSYNC, you make me rich by Brian Courtney, Ain't nothing going on but the rent by Gwen Guthrie, and Nothing from Nothing by Billy Preston. Calloway's, I Wanna to Be Rich has a message in the theme.

Locke, "Kevin O'Leary: If Elon Musk Pitched Tesla on 'Shark Tank,' 'I Would Have Said No.'"

Ciaccia, "Why Elon Musk Thought Tesla Would Fail."

Compulsions do not discriminate and are not focused socioeconomically, but a person with regular pay is much less likely to have a dependency than someone without industrial security. Years' worth of information indicates that addiction rates are two times as high among the unemployed as they are among the employed; in many instances, the stress of unemployment leads to substance abuse. Dependency additionally boosts the probability that someone will have issues getting employment, and this may result in job loss and even decreased profits. Being fired for process performance can make it trickier to locate new work. This overall strain increases the chance of substance abuse. This is considered one of many motives why it is urgent to get out of poverty at once. Supplying the records in addition to addiction simulation can trigger tactical empathy; that's an F.B.I. degree.

An Addiction Simulation (uni.edu)

If people are still resistant, then accept it and talk to people about it, even if, in all fairness, the person that you are talking to has never had to battle an addiction. We have all had to battle something. Unfortunately, certain people are sociopaths, while others are just miserable. No matter the reason, you must be able to just let people be people and know when to decide that enough is enough and you are going to remove this person from your life since y'all cannot co-exist. If it is someone who is not as close to you as you want and isn't as empathetic as you want, I wouldn't worry too much about it because it's a waste of time and because, in the end, the people who matter the most are those who are in our inner circle.

Campbell, "An Addiction Simulation."

"Addiction And Low-Income Americans."

Mathematical physics uses meticulous strategies to resolve issues inside physics, while computational physics makes use of numerical strategies to resolve bodily issues for which a quantitative idea already exists. Wait a minute What on earth is physics – that is, technological knowledge – doing in a book about financial literacy? Because arithmetic is the study of numbers and the various ways in which they're written, you should recognize that if you can comprehend the fundamentals of how physics works and what physics is, you may have crossover training on how to comprehend monetary literacy, for example.

While computational physics uses numerical techniques to tackle physical problems for which a quantitative concept already exists, mathematical physics uses painstaking methods to solve problems inside the realm of physics. Wait a moment. What does physics—technical expertise—have to do with a book about financial literacy? Since arithmetic is the study of numbers and the different ways in which they are expressed, you should be aware that if you can understand the principles of what physics is and how it operates, you may already have the knowledge necessary to understand financial literacy, for instance.

If you obtain something resembling a wave cycle in physics, you can graphically accompany mathematical repeat samples. Math and physics can cooperate, just as there are various sorts.

"Patterns."

"Financial Relativity (Your Experience Is Not Mine) - Northern Expenditure."

"The Different Fields of Physics."

Calling out Walmart

My total spiked from $8.81 to $28.81, and I was blocked from receiving a refund from Walmart; instead, I was notified by a team member that I would have to accept a gift card and go to another Walmart. The thief was able to easily pay for his goods with cash; I did not get to see a video of the perpetrator of this crime, and yet members of asset protection were afforded the privilege. I rejected the gift card because I learn from my mistakes and buying from Walmart was a far bigger mistake for me because I was suffering from a mental health flare up that caused me to race out of the store.

All of them were a professional, from the villain to the officer, and for worse or better, they all saw it as the only way to make a living. I saw my counselor afterwards, but we must take safety and wealth in this country more seriously than we do. This was abominable under any circumstances; I was told that the staff was supposed to clean up did not. What happens in your occupation when you do not do your job? How about if it resorted in lawlessness? Some security guard who did not get how Walmart works, mistook this for a city issue; however, let me state unequivocally that this is specifically about Walmart. You can name call, and you can fault me if you choose, but Walmart has a lot of problems besides their negligence in this case.

To your left is a wilted-looking old man. A Black man smoking a cigarette outside the church on a bench; to your right, a person jaywalking into oncoming traffic in the street is not hit by a car because of our radical driving methods aligning with the turf; in the center is a double-parked car; detours are everywhere; and loud music blares in the background at the most inopportune time. I know I have my own mental health battles and compartmental personality flaws, but even if these people had more money and this neighborhood ended up gentrified, would these folks be able to adjust astutely? They would just look like an abstract low life on a high-class block. Seeing vandalism and hearing a neighbor say someone went in his unlocked car does not undermine my experience because, unlike at Walmart, I am not going out of my way to the suburbs to unknowingly be a crime victim.

The crime scenes I have encountered have been milder, exceedingly rare, and have not affected me in such an intimately haunting way as that of the Walmart crime incident. A literary agent incorrectly referred to this book as "slander" without even knowing the meaning of the word.

That would be slander if I tried to author an entire book based on the crimes here, regardless of the statistics with which I personally have dealt. We certainly have better security in my luxury building than Walmart. Packages do not get stolen left and right while the building shrugs it off.

This is the kind of thing everyday people affiliate with Walmart whether they shop there or not, is this how you want to be seen and see fellow customers at Walmart? I am so happy they can no longer lump me in with these definitions.

Walmart

known for its awful public relations, slave wages and advantages that match, predatory pricing, use of affordable overseas labor to produce its items in international locations such as China, Korea, Philippines, Malaysia, Cambodia, Thailand, and Vietnam, and frequently using unlawful immigrants for filth less costly wages right here in the USA…all the whilst advertising and marketing it's phony patriotism. Known for its giant field like look and exceptional big parking plenty with no trees. Walmart is crowded with human beings who do no longer have the great hygiene and are regularly obese due to the immoderate junk meals they buy at Walmart. Perhaps one of the worst matters Walmart does is to go into an area, pressure out all different groups and then shut down, leaving the place decimated.

Walmart is the single biggest importer of overseas produced desirable in the USA. So, I bet that is what they imply when they say in their classified ads "Bringing it domestic to the USA"?

See this is part of why I wrote this book look at when that Walmart definition was made, October 28th, 2006, I was stolen from by another customer almost 16 years later to the day and there are more like this going back further, Walmart is a broken organization that is unredeemable.

I want to take a moment to segway for your benefit, perhaps you can utilize the following instead of shopping at Walmart.

Programming TI-84 Plus (Silvery Version) for Novices

https://www.instructables.com/Programming-TI-84-Plus-Silver-Edition-for-beginn/

You should commute to this site, Is your commute cost reasonable? Find out.

https://www.calculatorpro.com/calculator/commute-cost-calculator/

Do not get a speeding ticket. Average is fast enough. Look over here.

https://www.calculatorpro.com/calculator/average-speed-calculator/

Required Minimum Distribution

https://www.aarp.org/work/retirement-planning/required-minimum-distribution-calculator.html?cmp=KNC-DSO-COR-Retirement-23354-Bing-MinimumDistributionCalculator-Phrase-NonBrand&gclid=db8210ec93ac113c56407398c1ddf192&gclsrc=3p.ds&msclkid=db8210ec93ac113c56407398c1ddf192&utm_source=bing&utm_medium=cpc&utm_campaign=Core-Retirement-NonBrand-Phrase&utm_term=ira%20rmd%20calculator&utm_content=Minimum%20Distribution%20Calculator

"Urban Dictionary: Walmart."

I can't help but think about that white construction worker guy who answered an ad for a platonic friend on craigslist and was a Walmart customer with the Eurasian son and daughter and smoked how he left them to be stranded at Walmart over a cigarette when the motorist who had the best of intentions stood up to him and told him to get out, surely not all Walmart customers are that bad, I know I for one wasn't with that said it still makes you wonder what kind of communication Walmart is putting out that degenerates like that can't get enough of their store? , say what you want about the motorist but remember going there that day was that man's idea and he had been warned but the cigarettes were more important than the safety of his kids.

I worry about you can you imagine if this happened to you? The manager who followed up with me already admitted that the workers there were not doing their job and went against Walmart policy.

Walmart's Victim Audience

The target audience of Walmart is low to middle-class country families. These people want to shop conveniently in a specific location. The price and price cuts are something they look for while shopping. Walmart has been able to identify the target audience and created its stores as per the demand trends.

I saw a YouTube video which I could not even finish, this lady was warning ladies that they must watch out while in a Walmart parking lot. Both sexes must watch out in the Walmart parking lot as well as in Walmart because it is so dangerous. The biggest mistakes that the South ever made, alongside segregation based off skin color and the Confederacy which favored slavery for the benefit agriculturally was the decision to use that same agriculture to have so many God forsaken Walmart's put up where both whites and blacks and everyone else has to endure its existence which has to be third in line.

I was in that same type of parking lot sitting down in my car looking at a receipt with Cashback I didn't grab hold of as soon as it was ejected from the machine and panicking because I realized my money was left, if the crime could easily take place in the store near an employee who wasn't paying attention, what makes you think that you can be more secure than the Walmart loss prevention team? these videos keep being in Walmart parking lots for a reason.

"Walmart Marketing Strategy | Simplilearn."

It seemed surreal to me that an ordinary logical person like me would have to be persuaded after screaming to go outside and call the cops by a Hackensack cop, an off-duty police officer who introduced himself to me and who was also shopping there, that "we are not all idiots." He also said that to me the $20 being stolen was major, but to him it was minor, and nothing was being done unless the police were called, which I agreed with since obviously the staff had made matters much worse, and since there was no record of it, he urged me to make sure the theft was noted. Ask yourself this Is shopping for a day at Walmart worth a loss night's sleep? If you can still say absolutely, then you already have a huger issue going on than the alarming crime rate at Walmart and my traumatic theft combined. Shopping at Walmart is not worth your peace. It has been discovered that the United States has the highest economic loss from sleep deprivation in the world, losing about 292 percent of its total GDP to sleep deprivation. This equates to a 411, 10 to 9, or approximately 120000 workdays per year productivity loss.

Catmull, "Inc."

I was truly astounded when my cash was detracted from me at the store. It was truly obvious to me that one of the store workers was permitted to yell out during a gathering without thinking often about individuals close by. On the off chance that I had not failed to remember what occurred, I would have had the option to save money and not leave their more psychologically damaged than prior.

Walmart is where a great deal of things can be taken, like the lines for electric scooter cords that were stolen before this incident at another Walmart I went to and was informed of by team members, I ought to have been more cautious and not returned to Walmart after that occurred. I ought to have focused on consuming past that warning and keeping away from Walmart starting there on. Do you realize this has never happened to me at some other retailer? Truly, Walmart is more delicate, Walmart has such countless cheats in their stores that will take anything whenever so obviously I will undoubtedly be straightaway. Do you understand I had nothing like that happen to me in some other retailer? What occurred with Walmart is on the grounds that Walmart is more defenseless, jeopardizing its clients and workers by not valuing their safety.

In view of how Walmart treats long lasting clients, we can reason that individuals and their sentiments do not make any difference to them.

If it could happen to someone who owned a piece of Walmart through the stock market and had an online account with them, they do not mind if it happens to you, and you do not have to leave any money behind for it to occur.

In America and internationally, when one business closes another replaces it. Therefore, consumers must have faith in knowing that they will always have some place to shop.

Wal-Mart is not a standard merchandising store - neighborhoods are impacted in considerable ways by its ingress. Highly affected by intrusions. This whitepaper examines the Wal-Mart effect on crime using multiple data trails and multidimensional vulnerability modeling. Results for the 1990s converged, showing that Walmart is in a high crime U.S. County that has not implemented robust macroeconomic measures. When Walmart didn't take in crime, crime declined compared to matched counties The county's property crime rate dropped another 17 units per capita from the 1990s to the 2000s. A slightly statistically significant but stable effect of violent crime was also observed, decreasing by 2 units per person

I perceive Walmart as fake with fake signs, after my theft a lot came out, There wasn't any camera footage from the parking lot that was played.

There is no facial recognition technology which would lead to the capture of thieves all there are cameras on the self-check outs and possibly elsewhere.

The police officer said that this incident was treated the same as a shoplifting incident, how many shoplifters and law-abiding citizens alike see it that way? It really is a hot topic.

There is a lot of people who need to discover the truth about Walmart so please do the right thing and let them know. This is no different than when a person puts themselves in a dangerous situation and is a victim of crime, yes it was one of the biggest mistakes of my life, but I did not deserve it and now a criminal is on the loose ready to strike again.

Wolfe, Scott & Pyrooz, David. (2014). Rolling Back Prices and Raising Crime Rates? The Walmart Effect on Crime in the United States. British Journal of Criminology. 54. 2014. 10.1093/bjc/azt071.

My mom had told me that day to stay in the car,
should I have to stay in a dangerous parking lot to avoid going into a dangerous store? To some degree I wish I never went in the store that day, but I am grateful that I did. Of course, crime can happen anywhere which is beside the point, the point is your probability of being a victim of a crime while shopping goes down drastically when you decide to shop somewhere safer.
Just because the Federal trade commission can't stop Walmart doesn't make them anymore right, it makes them legal there is a distinction.
Walmart's unethical business practices are loosely similar to an unfair trade practice
in terms of targeting vulnerable populations, people shop at Walmart because either money is an issue for them monetarily or mentally.

Had I not gone in the store that day I would not have had the opportunity to become yet another victim at Walmart. I had to suffer so greatly and lose out immensely to know better about Walmart and warn you. I do not want you to hear from a customer service rep "Loss prevention saw what happened on tape, you left it, and someone took it." Coldly.

(The someone I later found out was a white middle-aged man with a family, who is where he is in life because he is yet another low life trying to live the high life on.)

regarding how asset protection saw the footage and then hear the same worker respond, " All I did was tell her." I could tell that all they wanted to do was silence me and remove me.

The Walmart monopoly has taken down many stores and can still be taken down, it is up to us to decide that we will not be pushed around and will push back when it comes to the excessive crime in Walmart stores. Empathize or else Walmart gets away with it. A Walmart manager told me that the team member was supposed to be cleaning and didn't follow Walmart policy and that they will have to do their jobs whether they like or not because they will be getting more self-check-out machines, they can't even update their tech or hold their staff accountable, he was just using programmed words.

My life has been so much better off since I stopped shopping at Walmart, and I can guarantee you that if you only would you would be able to say the same thing. I enjoy attentive staff elsewhere. I enjoy how when I go to Targets of which is not paying me to endorse them. How I must approve my money being withdrawn from the machine and how loud the alert is before it is all over. It does not matter whether you keep shopping at Walmart or not what matters is that you make sure you are safe and that you know that while you are shopping at Walmart you are missing shopping somewhere better. If I knew like I know now I would have never shopped there. I think about how much cleaner other stores are and I think about how much easier they are to navigate, and I have my confirmation of what I said that day to the manager on the phone. "Your company should not be in business." Or how I said to the worker, "You don't value money which is how come you work for Walmart." Those are tough words but what happened to me and keeps happening to other customers is tougher. The only difference between them and I, is I have the courage to write a saucy exposé. If I were a Walmart worker, I would not want to work somewhere that repays customers by being negligent.

CPSIA information can be obtained
at www.ICGtesting.com
Printed in the USA
LVHW102022060123
736479LV00002B/535

9 781685 836023